Further Ahead

A communication skills course

for Business English

Teacher's Guide

Sarah Jones-Macziola

CAMBRIDGE
UNIVERSITY PRESS

PUBLISHED BY THE PRESS SYNDICATE OF THE UNIVERSITY OF CAMBRIDGE
The Pitt Building, Trumpington Street, Cambridge, United Kingdom

CAMBRIDGE UNIVERSITY PRESS
The Edinburgh Building, Cambridge CB2 2RU, UK
40 West 20th Street, New York, NY 10011–4211, USA
477 Williamstown Road, Port Melbourne, VIC 3207, Australia
Ruiz de Alarcón 13, 28014 Madrid, Spain
Dock House, The Waterfront, Cape Town 8001, South Africa

http://www.cambridge.org

© Cambridge University Press 1998

This book is in copyright, which normally means that
no reproduction of any part may take place without
the written permission of Cambridge University Press.
The copying of certain parts of it by individual teachers
for use within their classrooms, however, is permitted
without such formality. To aid identification, pages
which are copiable by the teacher without further
permission are identified by a separate copyright
notice: ' Photocopiable © Cambridge University Press 1998'.

First published 1998
Fifth printing 2004

Printed in the United Kingdom at the University Press, Cambridge

ISBN 0 521 59784 6 Teacher's Guide
ISBN 0 521 53172 1 Learner's Book with CD ROM
ISBN 0 521 59785 4 Learner's Book Cassette
ISBN 0 521 63928 X Learner's Book CD
ISBN 0 521 59783 8 Home Study Book
ISBN 0 521 59782 X Home Study Cassette
ISBN 0 521 63929 8 Home Study CD
ISBN 0 521 58779 4 Video and Teacher's Guide (VHS PAL)
ISBN 0 521 58778 6 Video and Teacher's Guide (VHS SECAM)
ISBN 0 521 58777 8 Video and Teacher's Guide (VHS NTSC)
ISBN 0 521 62645 5 Video Activity Book

Contents

Map of the course

	Students will learn how to	Grammar points	Business content	Resource activities (Teacher's Guide)/ File Cards (Learner's Book)
UNIT 1	Introduce yourself and others Greet visitors Keep a conversation going Ask questions to find out more about people	**Questions** Question tags Question forms	Introductions, greetings, small talk	Introductions *Files 1 and 2 – Telephone call/info gap activity*
UNIT 2	Describe different types of companies Find out about companies Find out about a particular product	**Past time** Past simple – statements and questions **Irregular verbs** **Questions** *Who, What*, etc.	Vocabulary: kinds of businesses and industries Business letters and phone calls	Local industries My company *Files 3 to 6 – Telephone call/ info gap activities*
UNIT 3	Talk about company organization Draft an advertisement for a vacancy Talk about your job and its responsibilities Ask to speak to someone and to leave a message	**Present time** Past simple and present progressive	Vocabulary: departments and jobs within a company responsibilities of different jobs Business calls	*Files 7 to 10 – Taking telephone messages*
UNIT 4	Make and accept/reject invitations Talk about hobbies and interests Get information Talk about likes and dislikes	**Verb patterns** verbs followed by –ing **Adverbs of frequency**	Make social arrangements Market research	Find someone who … *Files 11 and 12 – Inviting a business associate to a social function*
UNIT 5 Revision and consolidation				
UNIT 6	Talk about infrastructure Describe facilities Compare advantages and disadvantages Deal with orders	**Comparative and superlative adjectives** **Adjectives describing quality** **Punctuation and capitalization**	Transportation of goods Types of cargo Writing faxes and memos	*Files 13 and 14 – Discussing and comparing transport facilities*
UNIT 7	Talk about imports and exports Talk about quantity Describe change: past and present	**Quantity** Mass and count nouns Expressions of quantity: a few, a little **Past time** Past simple and present perfect	Import and export industries Types of industries Trade between countries and what different countries produce	*Files 15 and 16 – Describing charts and diagrams*
UNIT 8	Talk about schedules Make and change arrangements and appointments Deal with correspondence Make a telephone call to arrange a meeting	**Future time** Present progressive and *will* future	Plan a business trip Discuss an itinerary Dealing with different kinds of correspondence and writing a fax Make and change appointments	*Files 17 and 18 – Discussing arrangements and an itinerary for a business trip* *Files 19 to 22 – Making and changing appointments for a business meeting*
UNIT 9	Describe a product Make and deal with complaints Apologize	**Adjectives** Materials/shapes/qualities	Banking and financial services Customer service: apologizing and providing information	*Files 23 to 26 – Dealing with a bank by telephone/providing good customer service* *Files 27 and 28 – Persuading someone to buy something*
UNIT 10 Revision and consolidation				

	Students will learn how to	Grammar points	Business content	Resource activities (Teacher's Guide)/ *File Cards (Learner's Book)*
UNIT 11	Discuss a company's image Talk about different ways of promoting a product Discuss the advantages and disadvantages of various forms of promotion	**Relative pronouns** *who, which*	Company image and promotional material Advertising a product Marketing Ordering promotional materials	Definitions
UNIT 12	Describe trends Talk about cause and effect Give reasons for changes in performance Discuss training programmes Make a short presentation	**Adjectives and adverbs** **Sequencing language**	Describe a business's performance In-house training programmes Making presentations	*Files 29 and 30 – Describing a graph* *Files 31 and 32 – Discussing product sales and giving reasons for increase/decrease* *Files 33 and 34 – Giving a short presentation/practise structuring a short talk*
UNIT 13	Take part in a business negotiation Write a letter chasing payment	**Conditionals** First conditional **Time clauses** *when* and *as soon as*	Negotiate prices and conditions Cash flow and debt problems Chasing letters	*Files 35 and 36 – Negotiating a sale* *Files 37 to 40 – Chasing payment/ giving reasons*
UNIT 14	Discuss different countries' attitudes to gift giving Making arrangements for a free day in a foreign city Discuss food and its preparation	**Indirect/polite questions** *Could you tell me where …*	Dealing with other cultures and customs Free time on a business trip Socializing in business	My home town
UNIT 15 Revision and consolidation				Cost of living guide
UNIT 16	Discuss a company's culture Express probability Give an opinion Express preference	**Modal verbs** *would/might/wouldn't*	Company culture Business ethics Women in business	Class survey *Files 41 – Women in work*
UNIT 17	Discuss green issues in the office Make recommendations Ask for an opinion and agree or disagree	**Reported speech** Reporting verbs	Business and the environment Budgets Business discussions	Be Green *Files 42 and 43 – Direct/indirect speech* *Files 44 to 47 – A company meeting to discuss budgets*
UNIT 18	Describe a process Describe a company's history Talk about work conditions	**Modals** *have to/must/can/don't have to/ can't/mustn't* **Passive** past and present	Production methods	Company history
UNIT 19	Case study: organizing a conference and giving a brief presentation		Conference organization: arrangements schedules Correspondence: invitations answering queries Make a presentation	*Files 48 and 49 – Arranging a conference at a hotel*
UNIT 20 Revision and consolidation				

Introduction

Further Ahead is a course for learners at lower intermediate level who want to improve their English for business and professional purposes. It is suitable both for learners who are pre-work and those already in employment. The *Learner's Book* contains 20 units, four of which are review units. It provides material for between 50 and 70 hours of classroom work. The units are topically based but incorporate practice in all four skills, as well as a balance between controlled practice and meaningful communication activities. The course provides a clear structural progression, which can be seen in the *Map of the course* on pages iv–v. This map also explains the functional coverage and business content of the course.

The components of *Further Ahead* are:

- Learner's Book
- Learner's Book Cassette
- Learner's Book CD
- Teacher's Guide
- Home Study Book
- Home Study Book Cassette
- Home Study Book CD
- Video and Teacher's Guide
- Video Activity Book.

The *Teacher's Guide*

The *Teacher's Guide* provides:

- detailed suggestions on how to exploit the material in the *Learner's Book*
- comprehensive support for those teaching Business English for the first time through to experienced teachers of Business English
- a full answer key
- complete tapescripts integrated into the notes as they occur in each lesson
- nine photocopiable *Resource activities*, to be used at the teacher's discretion. These activities supplement the *Learner's Book* content and are designed to be useful in a wide range of situations.

Organization of the *Teacher's Guide*

The different stages of each unit are categorized into one (or a combination) of the following:

- Warmer/Discussion
- Presentation
- Language focus
- Reading
- Listening
- Speaking
- Vocabulary
- Writing
- Resource activities.

These categories are used for each separate task throughout the *Teacher's Guide*, although they are not used in the *Learner's Book*, where the tasks are designated by sequential lettering only.

Warmer/Discussion

These activities act as mini-discussions for the class, eliciting vocabulary, introducing the topic and heightening learner awareness and interest.

Presentation

There is no standard means of presentation in the book: a variety of means is used, including reading, listening and vocabulary exercises. The *Teacher's Guide* contains suggestions for utilizing the presentation.

Language focus

Following the presentation, learners are given the opportunity to analyse new language and to practise it in a variety of ways, usually involving a written and/or listening exercise. Complete summaries of new grammar are also given at the end of each *Revision and consolidation* unit, and extra practice is given in the *Home Study Book*.

Reading

The reading texts and accompanying activities are designed to provide learners with achievable goals. Suggestions on the presentation and extension of the reading tasks are included in this *Teacher's Guide*. These tasks practise the main ways of reading – skimming and scanning, intensive and extensive reading.

Most reading texts have illustrations, charts or photographs that provide learners with a context which the teacher can use to prepare the learners for the reading. Proper contextualization of the text will help the learner complete the reading tasks successfully. The graphics also provide the teacher with possibilities for the extension of the topic or theme.

Listening

Listening presents problems for the majority of learners, not only for those at lower intermediate level. Plenty of practice is given in improving extensive and intensive listening skills, and full tapescripts are given in the *Learner's Book*.

Speaking

The speaking activities are initially very structured and supported but quickly give way to freer discussion-type activities. Many of the freer speaking activities involve the use of the role cards in the *Files* at the back of the *Learner's Book*. It is important that learners have prepared their role thoroughly before attempting these activities, as this will help them to complete the task with a feeling of success. Preparation with other learners who have the same role and drilling language components in these groups will help learners' confidence.

Vocabulary

Key vocabulary and exponents are listed in the *Summary* sections of the *Revision and consolidation* units. These sections also give learners the opportunity to build their own personalized vocabulary lists. Throughout the book, American English equivalents of specifically British English language items are given. Although *Further Ahead* has a strongly international focus, it follows British English models, unless the context is clearly North American.

Writing

The main aim in the writing exercises (and in the example correspondence appearing elsewhere in the book) is to provide models of common business correspondence and to make learners aware of the role of register. The writing tasks are often used as an extension or consolidation of the other skills, for example, learners might have to write a letter to follow up a role play of a telephone call.

Resource activities

These activities provide further practice in the relevant language points. They can also be used as warmers at the start of the next lesson or as revision exercises at a later point. They will be especially useful for classes where learners are pre-work or working in the same company.

Using the *Home Study Book*

The *Home Study Book* provides learners with an opportunity to continue their studies at home and to reinforce learning. The listening material on the separate cassette/CD also provides learners with a chance to develop and improve their listening skills at their own pace.

It will be beneficial, especially at the beginning of the course, to look at the *Home Study Book* with learners in class in order to introduce the different types of activities and to ensure that it is clear what they are expected to do. Learners can then complete the activities at home. Integrating the *Home Study Book* into your course will let learners see that it is an important part of *Further Ahead* and encourage them to work on their own, thereby maximizing their learning.

Video

Further Ahead video is linked thematically with the *Learner's Book*. The video presents the coursebook's themes in a fresh and authentic context through four specifically filmed documentary sequences, and provides excellent extension and revision material.

The video relates to the coursebook as follows:

Sequence 1: *Welcome to Prince*
- describing company organization
- telephoning
- talking about product innovation
- dealing with customers
- discussing company culture
(Units 1–4)

Sequence 2: *The Delivery*
- dealing with an order
- telephoning
- transportation
- making plans

(Units 6–9)

Sequence 3: *What's in a brand name?*
- describing product ranges
- comparing products
- dealing with customers
- talking about the past

(Units 11–14)

Sequence 4: *The Solar Way*
- describing a technical process
- defining market sectors
- demonstrating application of technology
- talking about the future

(Units 16–19)

The video is sold with an A5 *Teacher's Guide*, which has photocopiable tasks for learners. A separate *Video Activity Book* is also available.

1 People

This unit deals with introducing yourself and others, greeting visitors, keeping a conversation going and asking questions to find out more about other people. Question forms are reviewed, and question tags are introduced. As the main theme is meeting and greeting people, this unit provides a chance for you and the learners to get to know each other and develop group cohesion, which will be important in successfully completing tasks later in the book. Language input is fairly low at this point and the speaking and writing activities will provide you with a good opportunity to judge the level of your class.

Further Ahead Video Sequence 1, 'Welcome to Prince', covers the themes dealt with in Units 1 to 4 of the Learner's Book.

1.1 Meeting people

A Warmer

● Ask learners to look at the pictures in their books and tell you where the people are and if they think they know each other. Establish the context of introductions and greetings and elicit suggestions as to what the people could be saying. Write these on the board. Learners can compare them later with the listening in the next section.

● You could try to extend this step beyond the routine formula of introductions and greetings to include ideas as to how the conversations may continue, e.g.:

How are things …?
Did you have a good flight?
Where are you from?
Is this your first visit to …?
What do you do?

You will not need to go much beyond this as this is the topic of **1.2**.

B Listening and presentation

● Play the first dialogue and ask learners to decide which picture it goes with.

● Play it again and ask learners to listen for key phrases (e.g. *My name's …, Pleased to meet you*, etc.). Write these on the board and any alternatives which learners can provide.

● Proceed in the same way with the two remaining dialogues.

Answers
1c   2b   3a

 *Tapescript*

Conversation one
WOMAN 1: Hello. I don't think we've met. My name's Gina Lee.
MAN 1: And I'm Paolo Mendes. Pleased to meet you, Ms Lee.
WOMAN 1: Where are you from, Mr Mendes?
MAN 1: Brazil, Rio de Janeiro, to be exact. I work for Ark. Perhaps you've heard of them? I'm a software engineer there. And what about you? What do you do?
WOMAN 1: I'm in hardware development with Cor.
MAN 1: That's interesting. Perhaps you can tell me something about …

Conversation two
WOMAN 2: Wendy, do you know Dirk Dressler? Dirk, this is Wendy James from United Finance.
MAN 2: I don't think we've met before. Nice to meet you, Ms James.
WOMAN 3: How do you do? Please call me Wendy.
MAN 2: And I'm Dirk.
WOMAN 3: What exactly do you do, Dirk?
MAN 2: I'm responsible for quality control. I …

Conversation three
MAN 3: Hello Mikiko. Nice to see you again.
WOMAN 4: Hi Oscar. How are you?
MAN 3: Fine thanks. And you?
WOMAN 4: Oh, not too bad. How are things in Sydney?

MAN 3: Pretty good. We're quite busy at the moment. But I'll tell you about that later. Did you have a good flight?

WOMAN 4: Well, we were late taking off, but …

C Language focus

- Ask learners to look at the language boxes in their books. Read through the exponents and use them to practise pronunciation.

- Then give prompts and get learners to provide the correct responses, e.g.:

  T: *How do you do?*
  L: *How do you do?*
  T: *How are you?*
  L: *Fine, thanks.*
  T: …
  L: …

- Improvise one of the conversations with a learner, substituting information about yourself. Learners continue in twos and threes to practise the other two conversations, substituting their own information this time. If you feel it is appropriate, round up by asking one or two pairs to act out one of the conversations in front of the class.

D Speaking

This activity is a class survey.

- Ask learners to look at the questionnaire in their books and elicit the questions they need to ask other learners in order to complete the chart, e.g.:

  What's your name?
  What do you do?
  Where are you from?

- If your learners are all from the same country, substitute this with city.

- Demonstrate what learners should do by going up to one learner and introducing yourself before you ask the questions. Encourage them to use the language they have been practising in this section, e.g.:

  T: *I don't think we've met? My name's Simon Black.*
  L: *I'm Wolfgang Lotz.*
  T: *Pleased to meet you, Wolfgang.*
  L: *How do you do, Simon?*

- Give learners a few minutes to mingle with each other and interview four other

members of the group. Stop when you think the first ones have got this far. Learners then take it in turns to introduce a couple of the people they talked to to the rest of the class, using the prompts in their books as a help.

If your learners already know each other, use the Resource activity.

Resource activity 1: Introductions

The *Teacher's Guide* contains a number of extra Resource activities. In contrast to the Files, most of these are whole group activities and will involve a certain amount of moving around. There is no reference to these activities in the *Learner's Book*, so it is up to you to decide if and when you want to use them, e.g. you may feel that your learners need extra practice and use them to provide this, or they might be useful as a warmer to the next lesson after presenting the material. The photocopiable material is at the back of this book.

- Copy the cards at Resource activity 1, page 80, and hand them out.

- The aim of this activity is for learners to introduce themselves and ask questions about their partner – this is based on the listening at **1.1B**.

1.2 Keeping the conversation going

A Warmer

- Tell learners they will be dealing with a visitor to their company whom they are meeting for the first time. Elicit the kind of things they could talk about for the first few minutes before they start discussing business. Hopefully they will come up with topics such as the visitor's journey to the company, the hotel, etc. Note these on the board.

- In pairs, learners write down three questions they could ask a visitor in the situation outlined above. While they are doing this, go round and check their questions for both appropriacy and accuracy. This will give you an indication as to how your learners can cope with different tenses, question formation, etc.

- Stop the activity after a few minutes, even if your learners have not quite finished, and ask each pair to read out their questions. Write useful and/or common ones under the appropriate headings on the board.

B Listening and presentation

● Play the tape and ask learners to compare the questions they hear (from both the host and the visitor) with their questions. Then play it again, pausing for learners to write down the questions they hear.

Answers

1 Is this your first trip to …?
2 What do you think of it?
3 Do you live in …?
4 Which part of … are you from?
5 Have you ever been to …?
6 How long are you staying?

Tapescript

MAN: Are you Ms Novak?
WOMAN: Yes, that's right.
MAN: I'm Bruno Soares, the Sales Manager. How do you do?
WOMAN: How do you do? It's nice to finally meet you – to put a face to a name.
MAN: Yes, it is, isn't it? Now, come this way and we'll go up to my office. Is this your first trip to Porto?
WOMAN: Yes, it is. I've been to Lisbon a couple of times before, but this is the first time I've been to Porto.
MAN: And what do you think of it?
WOMAN: It seems like a nice place. Do you live in Porto itself?
MAN: No, I don't. I live to the north. It's about twenty minutes from here, depending on the traffic. And what about yourself? Which part of the States are you from?
WOMAN: The Midwest. From Omaha, Nebraska. Have you ever been there?
MAN: No, I haven't, unfortunately. How long are you staying in Porto?
WOMAN: Until Friday. And then I'm heading north. To Belgium.
MAN: Right, here we are. Now can I get you a drink before we start …

C Language focus

● If learners need pronunciation practice, drill the above questions from prompts, checking pronunciation and intonation as you go. Get learners to practise giving answers to the questions, making up information if necessary.

D Speaking

● Learners match each sentence with a picture.

Answers
1c 2a 3f 4d 5b 6e

● Then ask them to decide who says what (H = host; V = visitor; E = either) and to suggest a reply to each question.

Answers
1 Where are you staying?   [H]
2 Is the traffic always like this?   [V]
3 What do you think of the conference?   [E]
4 Do you work here in Paris?   [V]
5 Is it your first trip to New York?   [H]
6 Did you have a good flight?   [H]

Suggested answers
1 At the Hilton.
2 Unfortunately, yes. The rush hour starts at four.
3 It's very interesting.
4 No, I don't. I work in Lyon.
5 No, it isn't. I was here last year too.
6 Yes, thank you.

● In pairs, learners write a short dialogue based around one of these situations. Either let learners choose their own situation or, to ensure that learners work on different dialogues, number a set of cards from 1 to 6 and ask each pair to draw a card. This becomes their situation. The dialogue should incorporate about eight exchanges. If you wish to make it more of a challenge, set a limit to the number of words, e.g. 87.

● If you feel it is appropriate, ask learners to act out their dialogue once they have finished. If you think they will feel uncomfortable doing this, simply ask them to show their dialogue to another pair.

1.3 Finding out about people

A Reading

● Learners look at the form in their books and suggest what it could be for (magazine subscription).

● Put the headings from the subscription form on the board and elicit the questions learners need to ask you (i.e. second person) in order to complete the form, e.g. *What's your surname? What do you do? Who do you work for?* etc.

- In pairs, learners complete as much of the form as they can for Pamela Thomas. They will not be able to fill in how she wishes to pay as there is a choice between Mastercard and American Express. They will establish this from the listening in the next section. They will also find out her job title from the listening.

B Listening and presentation

- Learners complete the missing information, i.e. how Pamela Thomas wishes to pay and what her job title is.

  Answer
  Mastercard, Accountant

Tapescript

THOMAS: Pamela Thomas. Good morning.
CHANG: Good morning. This is Brenda Chang from Asia Business Publications. I'm calling about your subscription for *The Economist.*
THOMAS: Oh yes.
CHANG: I'm afraid your fax isn't very clear, so I'd just like to check some of the details.
THOMAS: Of course.
CHANG: Right. Your first name's Pamela, isn't it?
THOMAS: That's right.
CHANG: And you work for Extratour, don't you?
THOMAS: Yes.
CHANG: Now, I'm afraid I can't read your job title at all. What do you do, Ms Thomas?
THOMAS: I'm an accountant.
CHANG: Right. And I can't read the name of the street either.
THOMAS: That's Bourke Street. That's B-O-U-R-K-E.
CHANG: And that's in Melbourne, isn't it?
THOMAS: Yes, that's right.
CHANG: OK. Now, you want to pay by Mastercard, don't you?
THOMAS: Yes.
CHANG: Could you give me your account number?
THOMAS: Sure. It's 5412 0012 4567.
CHANG: Right then, I think that's everything. You should get your first copy in a couple of weeks.
THOMAS: Thanks very much.

- If your learners need the practice, ask them to role play the call, using their own information this time.

C Language focus

- Ask learners if they can remember how the caller checked Pamela Thomas's details. Write on the board the examples from the listening:

  Your first name's Pamela, …
  You work for Extratour, …
  That's in Melbourne, …

  and ask them to complete the sentences. If necessary, replay them.

- Then establish the rule that the auxiliary verb is repeated in the tag. If you have a positive statement, the tag is negative and vice versa. Note also the falling intonation to confirm information. Give a few more examples around the class, using information you have about your learners, e.g. names, companies they work for, etc. It is probably best to keep to the present tense while you are doing this, unless you feel confident that your learners can cope with more.

- In pairs, learners complete the task.

  Answers
  2 You work for McCash, *don't you?*
  3 You're the Assistant Manager, *aren't you?*
  4 You live in Portland, *don't you?*
  5 You're American, *aren't you?*
  6 You're not married, *are you?*

- Give them a few minutes to write down some things about other learners in the class and then let them check their information. If you have a large class, split learners into groups of five or six to do this.

D Speaking

- Learners practise asking and answering questions about a third person, i.e. Paul Harris or Sharon Willis, in the context of a telephone call. Divide the class into two groups. Group A looks at File 1 on page 117 and Group B looks at File 2 on page 120. Give them a few minutes to write down the questions they need to ask in order to complete their form and then regroup learners so that they are sitting with a person from the other group. In pairs they then exchange information. While they are doing this, go round and make notes on use of language to give feedback on once the activity has finished.

- To round up, ask questions around the class to ensure that the information is correct and then give feedback on use of language.

2 Talking about companies

Unit 2 deals with companies and products. Different lines of business are considered, and learners then work on questions to find out more about particular companies and products. The past simple for statements and questions is reviewed, together with irregular verbs and questions with *Who, What*, etc. Other points include a review of business letter style and a role play practising telephone calls to find out information.

2.1 Describing a company

A Warmer

- Start by giving learners the names of a few big, well-known companies and eliciting the line of business they are in, e.g.: Apple – computers, McDonalds – catering, etc.

- Ask learners to look at the list of industries in the box and think of other local examples. Use this as an opportunity to introduce and revise different lines of industry. Then ask your learners to match the company to a line of business. Make them do this fairly quickly and on their own in preparation for the discussion below.

B Language focus

- Draw learners' attention to the exponents in the speech bubbles and check they understand the differing degrees of certainty. Write on the board:

  100%   75%   50%
  I'm sure …   I think …   It could be …

- Point out ways of agreeing and disagreeing and then ask learners what line of business they think the first company is (or is not!) in and encourage them to give reasons. In small groups of three or four, learners compare their answers to the preceding task, e.g. I think Monterrey Taco Company could be a transport company.

  Answers
  Containex: packaging; Bars and Stripes: bar coding; Iced Meals: transport; Jupiter Sciences: aerospace; Bolshoi Trading: financial services; Monterrey Taco Company: catering.

📄 *Resource activity 2: Local industries*

- In pairs, learners write down the names of the ten biggest local companies.

- Then they join another pair and modify their lists so that they are in agreement.

- Finally, these groups modify their lists as a class. Once you have a 'definitive' list of the ten biggest local companies, establish which lines of business they are in.

C Reading

- Learners read the company profiles and match them with a name from **A**. In pairs or small groups, learners compare their answers using the exponents from **B**.

  Answers
  1 Jupiter Sciences
  2 Monterrey Taco Company
  3 Containex
  4 Bolshoi Trading

- Have learners reread the texts and underline the words which helped them find the answers. They can then compare their answers in pairs or small groups.

D Language focus

- Learners look at the questions and then try to find the answers in the text.

  Answers
  1 Atlas Copco Group
  2 compressor, construction and mining and industrial technologies
  3 Answer given on cassette: compressors and other equipment for mining and construction
  4 Over 21,000 world-wide
  5 Answer given on cassette: Stockholm, Sweden
  6 Answer given on cassette: European Union

- They then listen to the interview to check their answers and complete the missing information.

▭ ◎ *Tapescript*

INTERVIEWER:	What's the name of your company?
EMPLOYEE:	The Atlas Copco Group.
INTERVIEWER:	What line of business are you in?
EMPLOYEE:	We're in the mining and industrial sectors.
INTERVIEWER:	What goods or services does your company provide?
EMPLOYEE:	We make compressors and other equipment for the mining and construction industries.
INTERVIEWER:	How many employees does your company have?
EMPLOYEE:	Over 21,000 world-wide.
INTERVIEWER:	Where are your headquarters?
EMPLOYEE:	In Sweden, in the capital, Stockholm.
INTERVIEWER:	Where are your main markets?
EMPLOYEE:	Well, we operate world-wide, but our main market is the European Union.

- Before getting learners to practise the exchange of information, you may need to drill the question forms and practise falling intonation for *Wh-* questions.

- For additional practice, learners ask and answer questions about one of the companies in **A**.

Ⓔ Speaking

- If learners are from different companies, get them to exchange information in pairs, using the questions from the previous section and making notes on what they find out. If they are from the same company or pre-work, use the Resource activity.

🗎 *Resource activity 3: My Company*

- Photocopy the cards (Resource activity 3, page 81) and hand them out to pairs of learners. Give learners a few minutes to read the cards and think about language they will need. Remind learners to use the listening exercise as a model for their conversations.

2.2 Starting a business

Ⓐ Reading

- Learners scan the text to find out what kind of business Servcorp is in. Then ask them to reread the article and correct the statements.

    ### *Answers*
    1 Slater started her business in <u>Sydney</u>.
    2 Servcorp was <u>not</u> a success from the start.
    3 The first client was an <u>overseas</u> lawyer.
    4 Servcorp provides offices <u>and</u> staff.
    5 Servcorp <u>doesn't operate</u> in the <u>USA</u>.
    6 The company's turnover was <u>US$28m</u> last year.

Ⓑ Vocabulary

- Learners reread the article, looking for words which fit the definitions given.

    ### *Answers*
    a set up
    b business plan
    c temporary
    d facilities
    e expand

Ⓒ Language focus

- Ask learners to look at the box and remind them how to form questions and negatives in the past. Then give them a couple of minutes to read through the text and find the irregular verbs.

    ### *Answers*

be *was*	have *had*	make *made*
become *became*	get *got*	say *said*
do *did*	go *went*	think *thought*

- In pairs, learners write down their questions. Stop them after a few minutes and check their answers.

    ### *Suggested answers*
    2 Where was her first office?
    3 Who was her first client?
    4 What was her turnover last year?
    5 Why did she go to Japan?
    6 When did she go to Japan?

Ⓓ Speaking

- Working in the same pairs, learners write three more questions (in the past) to ask Joan Slater.

- Regroup learners so they are working with a new partner and get them to role play an interview with Joan Slater. Point out that if they do not have the answers to their partner's questions, they should make up the answers. While they are doing this, make a note of any errors to discuss with the class once they have finished the activity.

2.3 Getting product information

(A) Presentation

- Start with blank piece of paper and ask your learners what they would expect to find in a business letter. Try and elicit items such as the letterhead, reader's address, date, etc. List these on the board.

- Draw the outline of a page on the board and elicit where these components of the letter usually go. This also provides an opportunity to revise prepositions such as *on the right*, *at the top*, *above*, *below*, etc.

- Point out, if necessary, different ways of writing the date, in particular, that in American English (AmE) the month comes first (05.21.199-), whereas in British English (BE) the date comes first (21.05.199-).

- Ask learners to look at the letter in their books and decide what kind of letter it is, i.e. an enquiry. Alone or in pairs, they complete the task.

   Answer
   See below.

ELECTRONICS

Jaie Balmes 11
COL Los Morales
11510 Mexico D.F.
Mexico

ABC Computing
F8, no 142, Min-Chaun E. Rd.
Sec. 3 Taipei
Taiwan

May 21, 199–

Dear Sir or Madam:

I saw your advertisement in this month's issue of *Asia-Pacific Computing World* and would like to receive more information on your range of electronic components.

I look forward to hearing from you.

Truly yours

M. A. Park

M. A. Park (Ms)
Sales Manager

Photocopiable © Cambridge University Press 1998

B Writing

- Elicit what you might send the writer of the letter, e.g. brochures, price lists, catalogues, references, samples, etc.

- Elicit suggestions as to how learners can complete the phrases in their books.

Suggested answers

1 Thank you for your letter of *May 21* | *enquiring* / *asking* | *about our products.*

2 We enclose
  We are pleased to enclose
  We have pleasure in enclosing | *our latest catalogue and price list.*

3 Please contact me *if you need any further information.*

- Make sure learners realize they will be writing to Ms Parks and point out the change in the opening and closing salutations if we know the name of the reader:

Reader unknown	Reader known
Dear Sir or Madam (AmE)	Dear Mr/Ms ...
Dear Sir or Madam (BE)	
Truly yours (AmE)	Sincerely yours/ Best regards (AmE)
Yours faithfully (BE)	Yours sincerely (BE)

In pairs, learners draft a reply on a blank piece of paper, paying attention to the layout of their letter. When they have finished, ask them to show their letter to another pair and to get their comments on it.

Answer

See below.

C Listening and presentation

- It is probably advisable to revise spelling at this point. A quick dictation to warm learners up or alert them to letters which may cause difficulty may be a good idea before you tackle the listening.

- Play the first phone call and ask learners to complete as much information as they can. They should compare their answers with a partner before listening a second time.

- Check their answers before proceeding in the same way with the second call.

ABC COMPUTING

F8, no 142, Min-Chuan E. Rd Sec. 3 Taipei Taiwan

Ms M. A. Park
Sales Manager
X Electronics
Jaie Balmes 11
COL Los Morales
11510 Mexico D.F.
Mexico

May 28, 199-

Dear Ms Park:

Thank you for your letter of May 21, enquiring about our products.

We enclose our latest catalogue and price list and hope you will find it of interest.

Please contact me if you need any further information.

Best regards,

...

Sales Manager

Photocopiable © Cambridge University Press 1998

Answers

Paul Reiner
AFC
524 West Capitol Street
Little Rock
Arkansas 72601

Erica Andersen
TAZ Technologies
24 Otis Street
San Francisco
California 94103

 Tapescript

Call one

TONG: ABC Computing. Good morning.

REINER: Oh, good morning. This is Paul Reiner from AFC. I'm interested in your *Vu-Tec* filters.

TONG: I'll send you our brochure. Could I have your name and address?

REINER: Sure. My name's Paul Reiner. That's R-E-I-N-E-R.

TONG: R-E-I-N-E-R.

REINER: And my address is AFC, 524 West Capitol Street in Little Rock, Arkansas.

TONG: Right. And the zip code?

REINER: 72601.

TONG: 72601. OK. I'll mail you a brochure today, Mr Reiner.

REINER: Thanks very much.

TONG: You're welcome.

Call two

TONG: ABC Computing. Good morning.

ANDERSEN: Could you send me some information about your *Vari-X* filters?

TONG: I'll send you our brochure. Could I have your name and address?

ANDERSEN: Sure. My name's Erica Andersen. That's A-N-D-E-R-S-E-N.

TONG: A-N-D-E-R-S-E-N.

ANDERSEN: And my address is TAZ Technologies. 24 Otis Street.

TONG: Sorry. Could you please spell the name of the street for me?

ANDERSEN: Otis. That's O-T-I-S. San Francisco. California 94103.

TONG: 94103. OK. I'll put a brochure and price lists in the mail today, Ms Andersen.

ANDERSEN: Thanks very much.

TONG: You're welcome.

D Speaking

● This is the first of a number of guided dialogues which occur in *Further Ahead*.

● Go through it with your class, eliciting the various alternatives and then practise the whole dialogue with one learner. Divide learners into pairs and get them to practise the dialogue with a partner until they feel confident.

● If necessary, write a model with exponents on the board like this:

ABC computing. Good morning.

I'm interested in Could you send me some information about	the *Vari-X* filters. your *Vu-Tec* line.

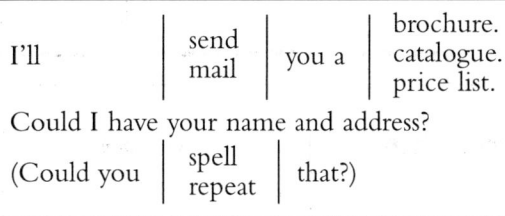

I'll	send mail	you a	brochure. catalogue. price list.

Could I have your name and address?

(Could you	spell repeat	that?)

Yes, it's *name and address*.

Right. I'll mail it today.

Thank you very much.

9

3 Jobs

In this unit, on *Jobs*, company structure and job responsibilities are dealt with, and tasks for learners include writing a job advertisement and practising taking and leaving telephone messages. Present simple and present progressive are reviewed, contrasting the everyday with a present activity.

3.1 Company structure

A Vocabulary

- As a warmer, put learners into groups of three or four and give them two minutes to brainstorm job titles. Stop them and ask them to compare their answers with another group after this time, thus extending their lists, or discuss the answers in a plenum, writing jobs on the board.

- Elicit some of the departments found in a typical company and their roles and write these on the board. Learners can then complete the first missing row of the organigram in their books.

- Ask learners to look at the list of jobs in the box. Can they assign them to the different departments? Learners can then complete the final missing row of the organigram in their books.

  N.B. Names of jobs and the departments people are assigned to vary from company to company, so if your learners have work experience, you may find them suggesting other titles for jobs or assigning them to different departments to the ones in the organigram here.

- You might want to focus on the words that actually carry the status of the job, e.g. clerk vs. officer.

- They will then check their answers in the listening in **B**.

  Answer
  See below.

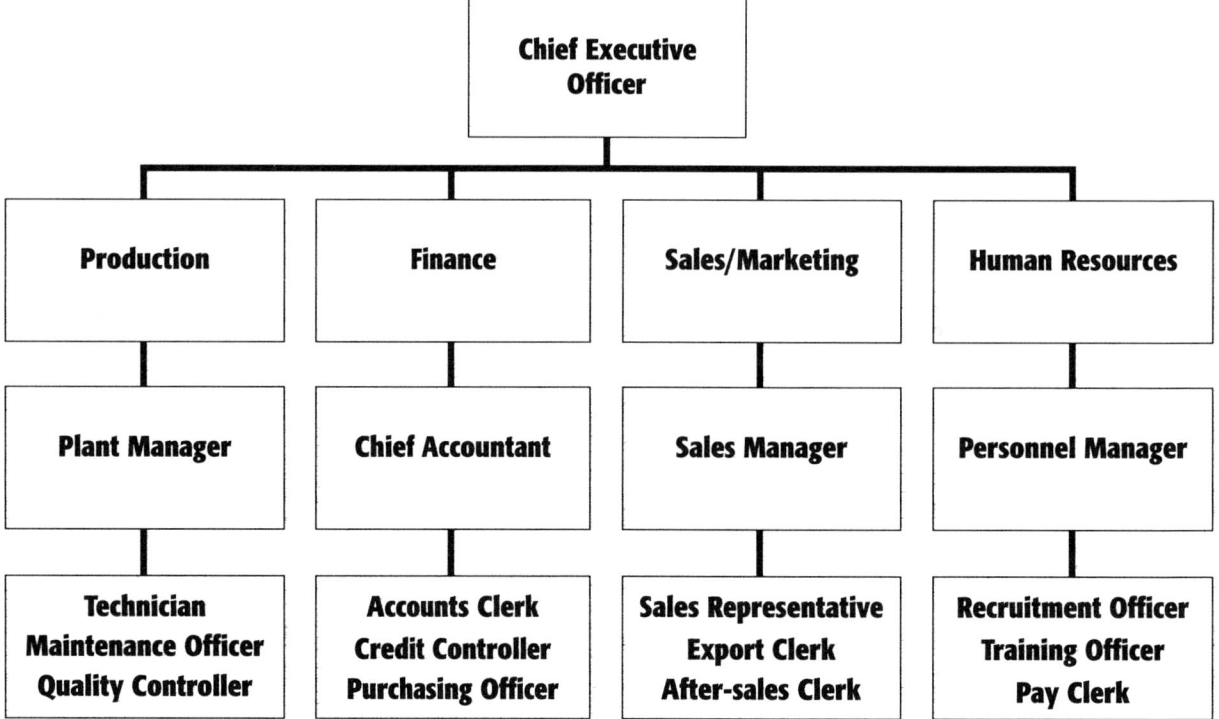

Production	Finance	Sales/Marketing	Human Resources
Plant Manager	Chief Accountant	Sales Manager	Personnel Manager
Technician Maintenance Officer Quality Controller	Accounts Clerk Credit Controller Purchasing Officer	Sales Representative Export Clerk After-sales Clerk	Recruitment Officer Training Officer Pay Clerk

Photocopiable © Cambridge University Press 1998

B Listening

- Learners listen to check their answers to the previous task.

🔊 ⊚ *Tapescript*

Now today I'll start off by telling you a little about the structure of Comex Xpress. The head of the company here in Glasgow is the CEO or Chief Executive Officer, and that's Mr Bateman.

Now, as you know, Comex Xpress is divided into four divisions: Production, Finance, Sales and Human Resources. The first division here is Production and that is headed by the Plant Manager, Tom McEwan. The Technicians, Maintenance Officers and Quality Controllers all report to him, as do the Packaging and Dispatch Clerks.

The next division is Finance and this department is headed by the Chief Accountant, Joshua Goldfinger. The Accounts Clerks and Credit Controllers, who check that customers have settled their invoices, report to him as does the Purchasing Officer.

Then we come on to the Marketing division which is both sales and marketing. The head of Marketing is Ms Julie Nicolson. She's responsible for the Export Clerks, the Sales Representatives who are on the road, and After-sales Clerks who deal with any problems that arise with our products.

Finally we have the Human Resources department, headed by Sheila Barrett. You met the Recruitment Officer Fiona Lewis at your interviews. Then there's myself, the Training Officer and finally the Pay Clerk, Ian Weir, so if you have any queries about salaries and so on you should go and see him …

C Reading

- Elicit the information learners expect to find in a job advertisement, i.e. skills and qualifications needed by the applicant, description of working conditions, etc.

- Ask them to identify and <u>underline</u> the expressions and phrases describing them in the two advertisements. Then ask them to suggest the positions they think are being advertised.

Suggested answers
1 receptionist
2 sales representative

D Writing

- Write the three headings on the board and ask learners to look at the first advertisement again. Categorize the information under the three headings like this:

  Your company
  Advertising agency

  Skills and qualifications
  keyboard skills
  pleasant telephone manner
  ability to deal with clients

  Working conditions
  attractive salary
  pleasant work environment

- Individually, or in pairs if you prefer, learners make notes on the job under the headings provided. They then draft an advertisement for their assistant.

- Ask pre-work learners to write an advertisement for a job they would like to have. They should think of it in terms of the skills they would need.

- Upon completion, circulate the advertisements and ask learners to decide which jobs they think are the best and worst!

3.2 Describing responsibilities

A Speaking

- Recap the departments mentioned in the last section and elicit some more, e.g. Dispatch, After-sales, etc.

- Ask learners to read the speech bubbles and guess which departments the people work in.

B Listening and presentation

- Play the tape once through before asking learners to complete the chart. Then replay it in segments, pausing after each speaker to give them time to fill in the chart.

Answers

Speaker	Department	Current projects
Frank	Accounts	*Sending reminders to slow payers*
Suzanne	Human Resources	Planning the training programme for next year
Peter	*Technical Services*	Preparing for a trade fair
Uschi	Marketing	Running a training course for the new sales reps
Rolando	Purchasing	Looking for a new supplier of office furniture
Elke	EDP	Testing new software for the sales force

Tapescript

Interview one

INTERVIEWER: What do you do, Frank?

FRANK: I work in Accounts. I'm responsible for invoicing our customers.

INTERVIEWER: And what are you doing at the moment?

FRANK: I'm sending out reminders to all our customers who haven't settled last year's invoices yet.

Interview two

INTERVIEWER: Tell me something about your work, Suzanne.

SUZANNE: I work in Human Resources. I'm in charge of training, er that's both for new employees such as school leavers and for employees who have already been here a while. I find trainers, organize venues, things like that.

INTERVIEWER: And what are you doing at the moment?

SUZANNE: Right now I'm planning the training programme for next year.

Interview three

INTERVIEWER: What do you do, Peter?

PETER: I work in Technical Services. We deal with customer problems, er, provide customers with spare parts, repair machines that break down, that kind of thing.

INTERVIEWER: And what are you doing at the moment?

PETER: Well, the company has just launched a new machine, so I'm actually preparing for a trade fair.

Interview four

INTERVIEWER: What do you do, Uschi?

USCHI: I work in Marketing. I answer customers' questions about our products. I also travel a lot, I give product presentations to our customers.

INTERVIEWER: And what are you doing at the moment?

USCHI: I'm running a training course for the new sales reps.

Interview five

INTERVIEWER: Tell me something about your work, Rolando.

ROLANDO: I work in the Purchasing Department. I'm responsible for buying everything the company needs – from ball-point pens through to the raw materials and components we need to make our products.

INTERVIEWER: And what are you doing at the moment?

ROLANDO: Well, people in Accounts have asked for some new chairs, so I'm looking for a supplier of office furniture.

Interview six

INTERVIEWER: What do you do, Elke?

ELKE: I work in EDP. I'm in charge of software development and maintenance. I also run a hotline for our employees if they have problems with their computers or programs.

INTERVIEWER: And what are you doing at the moment?

ELKE: I'm testing some new software for our sales force.

C Language focus

- Write on the board:

  I send invoices to customers.
  I'm sending invoices/reminders to slow payers.

  and ask learners if the two sentences mean the same. Elicit that the present simple is used for facts, frequently with time markers such as *often, sometimes, never,* etc., whereas the present progressive is used to refer to activities taking place now and currently (time markers – *now, at the moment*).

- From the speech bubbles in **A** and their notes from the listening, learners now write twelve sentences about the people at Acme International.

- For oral practice, elicit the two question forms, i.e. *What does X do? What's s/he doing at the moment?* Use them as prompts to talk about the people at Acme International.

D Speaking

- Set a limit of about five minutes for learners to take notes on their own jobs. It is probably useful to stipulate the number of things they should write down, for example five things that their job entails and two projects they are currently involved in. While they are doing this, you will probably need to go around helping with job-related vocabulary.

- In pairs, learners exchange information. Encourage them to take notes at this stage so they can report back to the class on their partner when they have finished.

3.3 Leaving a message

A Presentation and listening

- Ask learners to look at the messages and suggest which departments the people being called work in.

  ### Suggested answers
  1 Accounts
  2 Sales

- Play the first phone call and ask learners to underline any information which is not correct. Play it again and ask them to correct this information.

- Proceed in the same way with the second phone call.

Answers
(Incorrect information is underlined. Correct information is in brackets.)

GIZMO GADGETS MESSAGE

For: Stephanie Crooke
From: Hugh <u>Paine</u> (Payne)

Please send the list of last month's payments to head office by Friday, <u>13th</u> (14th).

GIZMO GADGETS MESSAGE

For: Stephen Stern
From: Tanya Cordrey

Please call about order no. <u>3574</u> (3754) tomorrow before 9 a.m. on <u>293 554</u> (293 544).

Tapescript

Call one

RECEPTION: Gizmo Gadgets. Good morning.

CALLER 1: Oh, good morning. This is Hugh Payne from Head Office speaking. Could you put me through to Stephanie Crooke in Accounts, please?

RECEPTION: Hold the line, please … I'm afraid the line's engaged. Would you like to leave a message?

CALLER 1: Er, yes, please. Could you ask her to send the list of last month's payments to head office by Friday the fourteenth at the latest?

RECEPTION:	Last month's figures to head office by Friday, the fourteenth. Who's calling, please?
CALLER 1:	Hugh Payne. That's P-A-Y-N-E.
RECEPTION:	Right, Mr Payne. I'll give Ms Crooke the message.
CALLER 1:	Thanks very much.
RECEPTION:	You're welcome.

Call two

RECEPTION:	Gizmo Gadgets. Good morning.
CALLER 2:	Hello. This is Tanya Cordrey from EKS. I'd like to speak to Stephen Stern in Sales.
RECEPTION:	Hold the line, please … I'm afraid he's in a meeting until 12. Can I take a message?
CALLER 2:	Oh, yes. Mm. Could you ask him to call me about my order, that's order number 3754, either sometime today or tomorrow before nine?
RECEPTION:	Order number 3754, today, or tomorrow before nine. Who's speaking, please?
CALLER 2:	Tanya Cordrey, from –
RECEPTION:	Sorry, could you spell that please?
CALLER 2:	Sure. That's C-O-R-D-R-E-Y.
RECEPTION:	C-O-R-D-R-E-Y. And your telephone number?
CALLER 2:	293 544.
RECEPTION:	Right, Ms Cordrey. I'll give him the message.
CALLER 2:	Thank you.
RECEPTION:	You're welcome.

B Listening and writing

- Before they listen, draw learners' attention to the way the messages have been written in **A**. Put the following model on the board:

  Please call (name) about (what) on (telephone number) before/after (time).

- The first time learners should just listen to the phone call and not write anything. Collect ideas (whether right or wrong) on the board. Then let them listen a second time and write the message afterwards. The completed pad should look like this.

Answer

GIZMO GADGETS MESSAGE

For: Mr Brunner
From: Rosie Grunwald

Please call her about the computer workshop for the marketing department on 665 433.

🔊 ◎ *Tapescript*

RECEPTION:	Gizmo Gadgets. Good morning.
CALLER:	Hello. This is Rosie Grunwald from Bit and Byte. I'd like to speak to Mr Brunner.
RECEPTION:	Hold the line, please … Hello. I'm afraid there's no reply. Would you like to leave your name and number, and I'll get him to call you back.
CALLER:	Oh, thank you. My name's Rosie Grunwald. That's G-R-U-N-W-A-L-D. Could you ask him to call me back about the computer workshop for the marketing department? My number's 665 433 and –
RECEPTION:	Sorry, what was the number?
CALLER:	665 433.
RECEPTION:	I'll just repeat that. Call Rosie Grunwald on 665 433 about the computer workshop for the marketing department.
CALLER:	That's it. Thanks a lot.
RECEPTION:	You're welcome.

C Language focus

- Ask learners if they can remember any of the way things were said in the phone calls, for example, how the callers asked to speak to the person they wanted to talk to, how the receptionist asked if they wanted to leave a message, etc.

- Go through the boxes to summarize and to check pronunciation.

- Then ask learners to look through the cues and go through the guided dialogue eliciting suggestions for each line. First practise it with a learner yourself and then in open pairs to make sure everyone understands what they are meant to be doing.

- In closed pairs, learners practise with a partner. Encourage the person taking the call to elaborate on the reason for Josie Williams not being available and for the caller to be more specific about the time when the call should be returned.

  You could also get learners to leave their own messages.

- If your learners need further practice, ask them to role play the calls from the messages in **A**.

ⓓ Speaking

- Divide learners into two groups and ask them to look at their respective file cards. Give them a few minutes to prepare what they want to say and then regroup learners into pairs.

- When they have finished the first role play, give them a few minutes to prepare again before they start the next role play.

- Listen in and make a note of good and bad use of language to give feedback on when the activity is finished.

4 Work and play

This unit, on the theme of *Work and play*, deals with making, accepting and rejecting invitations, talking about hobbies and interests and getting information for market research. Expressing likes and dislikes is also dealt with. Adverbs of frequency are introduced and practised.

4.1 Inviting

A Warmer

- Ask learners to look at the artwork in their books and establish what the various activities are. Tell learners they are going on a business trip to Sydney and ask them what they would like to do in their free time.

B Listening and presentation

- Learners listen to three conversations. Play them through and establish what the invitations are for. The second time learners should listen for whether the invitation is accepted or declined.

Answer

	Invitation	Reply
1	dinner	✗
2	barbecue	✓
3	harbour cruise	✓

▭ ◎ *Tapescript*

Conversation one

CAREY: Would you like to have dinner with me tonight?

HAWLEY: That's very nice of you, but I'm afraid I'm still a little jet-lagged from my trip and I'd like to make it an early night.

CAREY: Perhaps some time later in the week?

HAWLEY: Yes, that would be nice. Thank you.

Conversation two

CAREY: We're having a barbecue at my place on Wednesday. Would you like to come?

HAWLEY: Yes, that sounds great. I'd love to. What time?

CAREY: Around seven o'clock. Er, would you like me to arrange for someone to pick you up from your hotel?

HAWLEY: That's very nice of you. Thanks a lot.

Conversation three

CAREY: Do you have any plans for the weekend?

HAWLEY: Well, I thought I might do a little sightseeing, I haven't had time to see much of Sydney yet.

CAREY: Well, how about a harbour cruise on Saturday? You get a fantastic view of the city.

HAWLEY: That would be great. I'd love that.

CAREY: Good. I'll get some tickets.

C Language focus

- Ask learners if they can remember how the man made the invitations and how the woman accepted or declined them. Either write the exponents on the board if learners can give them to you or ask them to look at the language boxes in their books. Practise saying them, paying attention to intonation.

- Ask learners to look through the cues and go through the guided dialogue eliciting suggestions for each line. First practise it with a learner yourself and then in open pairs to make sure everyone understands what they are meant to be doing.

- In closed pairs, learners practise making and responding to invitations, using the pictures from **A** as cues.

D Speaking

- Divide learners into two groups and ask them to look at their respective file cards. Give them a few minutes to prepare what they want to say and then regroup learners into pairs.

- Listen in and make a note of good and bad use of language to give feedback on when the activity is finished.

4.2 Getting to know you

A Warmer

● Ask learners to look at the two comments. Establish how they rate the importance of social relations in business relations: in some countries, for example, business relations are based on social relations.

B Vocabulary

● Elicit ways people get to know each other better such as finding common interests, etc. Ask learners to look at the illustration and check they can name all the activities.

● To help build up vocabulary, put learners into small groups of three or four and then write *Sports* on the board. Give them two minutes to write down the names of as many sports as possible in their groups.

   N.B. play + ball games (football, golf, tennis)
   go + activity (cycling, sailing, swimming)

● Proceed in the same way with the following topics: *Books, Films, Music.*
   If you are short of time, divide your class into groups and assign each group a different topic. At the feedback stage, other groups can add any other ideas they have.

   Suggested answers
   Books: biography, detective, novel, science fiction, travel, etc.
   Films: action, comedy, horror, science fiction, westerns, etc.
   Music: classical, jazz, blues, pop, etc.

C Listening and presentation

● The first time, learners should just listen for the leisure activities mentioned: the second time they can complete the grid in their books.

   Answers

	M	W
Mountain biking	✗	
Gardening		✗
Jogging		✗
Sailing	✗	
Cinema		✗
Reading		✗

⏸ ◎ *Tapescript*

WOMAN: Well, I think the meeting went well today.

MAN: Yes, it did. But it's good to have a break from business.

WOMAN: So what do you do when you're not working?

MAN: Well, as I sit at a desk most of the day, I like to try and keep fit. I do quite a lot of sport.

WOMAN: Oh, yes. What do you do?

MAN: I enjoy cycling. Mountain biking actually.

WOMAN: I suppose it's a good place to do it here.

MAN: Yes, it is. And I've just taken up sailing.

WOMAN: Really? I didn't know there was any water around here.

MAN: Well, there's a couple of lakes nearby. But I prefer to go away – weekend breaks. What about yourself? Do you do any sports?

WOMAN: Well, I try and go jogging a couple of times a week. But I'm not really interested in sports. I love gardening. Otherwise I prefer to relax. I love going to the cinema. And I'm a real bookworm.

MAN: Really. What kind of things do you like reading?

WOMAN: Well, there's nothing that beats a really good murder!

MAN: You don't look the type for that!

WOMAN: Oh, you'd be surprised …

D Language focus

● Ask learners if they can remember any of the expressions used in the conversation above. Then ask them to look at the cline in their books, showing the various degrees of enjoyment and interest. Point out the use of *quite* and *not really* to modify the expressions and the use of the gerund after all these items. It is probably useful to contrast the use of *like + gerund* and *would like + infinitive* from **4.1**. You might also introduce a couple of expressions to express intense dislike of an activity, e.g. *I hate …; I can't stand … .*

- Get learners to give examples of their own of what they like and don't like doing in their leisure time. Don't spend too long on this. Give prompts by showing them pictures of leisure activities and asking them to comment on them, e.g.:

  Learner 1: I like jogging.
  Learner 2: I can't stand jogging.
  Learner 3: I quite enjoy jogging.

- Ask learners to look at the questions in their books. In pairs, they can interview their partner. If you wish to make the activity more of a challenge, get them to find three things they both like doing and three things neither of them like doing. Give them about five minutes to do this and then ask each pair to report back to the calls. Write on the board:

  Both of us …
  Neither of us …

Resource activity 4: Find someone who …

The object of the activity is for learners to find a different person for each activity; this means they can only use each learners' name once. Once someone has replied *yes* to a question, they should move on and talk to another learner.

- Give each learner a copy of the questionnaire (see Resource activity 4, page 82), or make a similar one tailoring it to your group's interests. Check they know what questions they should be asking. Make sure, in particular, that the questions are appropriate, for example, no. 1 *Do you have any family?* is more fitting than going straight in with *Do you have more than two children?*; also, for no. 5 we would ask a positive rather than a negative question, i.e. *Are you interested in sport?*

- Ask the whole class to stand up and give them about ten minutes to interview as many people as possible. Then stop the activity and ask various members to report back on what they found out. Encourage them, while they are doing this, to give more information where appropriate, e.g:

  Salwa has an unusual hobby. She plays women's rugby.
  Fatima plays an instrument. She plays the flute.
  Hassan has read a good book. It was … .

4.3 Market research

(A) Warmer

- Introduce the topic by asking learners if they have ever been interviewed by market researchers and, if so, for what products. Find out also what type of questions they were asked.

- In pairs, learners match the products to a potential customer.

  Suggested answers
  1e   2a   3c   4b   5d

(B) Reading

- Check that learners are familiar with the adverbs of frequency on the questionnaire before you begin the task. Either write these adverbs (jumbled) on the board or put them on cards and ask learners to arrange them in order of descending frequency they express, i.e. in the order on the form. Elicit any other ones your learners know which are not on the form and ask a few questions to check you are all in agreement as to their meaning. For example, how often do people do these things if they say: *I frequently go on business trips; I seldom make phone calls to the USA; I sometimes take clients out to lunch.*

- Give learners a couple of minutes to scan the questionnaire and establish the product the company is researching.

  Answer
  Notepad computer (c)

- Then ask them to study the questionnaire and decide if the person being interviewed is a potential customer or not.

  Answer
  Probably not

(C) Listening

- Learners complete the questionnaire, using the information from the tape.

Answer

Age: 15–18 19–24 25–34 35–49 50–64 65+ Sex: M/F						
	1	2	3	4	5	6
Travels for business	✗					
Works at home						✗
Gives presentations			✗			
Does own typing	✗					
Uses computer at work	✗					
Buys computer magazines						✗
(1 = regularly; 2 = frequently; 3 = often; 4 = sometimes; 5 = seldom; 6 = never)						

Photocopiable © Cambridge University Press 1998

Tapescript

INTERVIEWER: Excuse me. I'm doing some market research. Can I ask you a few questions?

WOMAN: Yes, of course. Go ahead.

INTERVIEWER: Right. Do you travel for business?

WOMAN: Yes, I do. On average I'd say I spend two or three days a week visiting customers.

INTERVIEWER: Right … 'regularly'. Now, do you ever work at home?

WOMAN: No, I don't. I'm so seldom at home, I don't want to have to work there too!

INTERVIEWER: OK. Next question. Do you ever make presentations?

WOMAN: Yes, I do.

INTERVIEWER: How often do you do that?

WOMAN: Let me see. Two or three times a month maybe. Some months it's more, some months it's less.

INTERVIEWER: Right. Let's say … 'often'. Now, do you usually do your own typing?

WOMAN: I'm afraid so. I don't have anyone to do it for me.

INTERVIEWER: OK. And do you use a computer at work?

WOMAN: Sure. I'd be lost without it!

INTERVIEWER: OK, I'll mark that 'regularly'. Do you ever buy computer magazines?

WOMAN: No, I don't. Never.

INTERVIEWER: Right. And one last question … Could you just look at this and tell me which age bracket you're in …

● Depending on the time you have available and on whether you feel your class needs practice with question forms, you could ask your learner to interview each other on the basis of the questionnaire in their books.

D Writing and speaking

● Put learners into small groups for this task. Set a time limit of about 15 minutes for formulating the questions. While they are doing this, go round the groups helping and checking that their questions are correct.

● Once they have finished, ask each learner to interview two or three other learners and then to report back to their group on what they found out.

5 Revision and consolidation

This is the first of four revision and consolidation units in the *Learner's Book*. They are intended to provide a skills-based revision and practice of the language covered in the previous four units. They should give a clear sense of learner's progress, and of areas that might need further attention. All four have a standard pattern: A Grammar – students analyse and correct faulty sentences; B What do you say? – matching functions to sentences; C Vocabulary; D Reading; and E Listening. A two-page summary, providing a grammar section and key vocabulary list, completes each consolidation unit.

A Grammar

This exercise reviews the main grammar points in Units 1 to 4.

● Give learners about 10 to 15 minutes to work through the sentences, correcting the mistakes. It is probably best if they do this in twos or threes, as it will encourage discussion of the mistakes and how they should be corrected.

● Then go through the sentences together, establishing what is wrong and how the mistakes can be corrected.

Answers
a   Joachim is **an** engineer.
b   He work**s** in the Frankfurt office.
c   You work for IBM, **don't** you?
d   Did **you have** a good journey?
e   I start**ed** working at this company when I left school.
f   When **did you join** the company?
g   Did you **go** to last year's sales conference?
h   Anita works in After-sales – she **deals** with customer complaints.
i   We**'re** develop**ing** a new model at the moment.
j   Would you like **to see** the factory after lunch?
k   Are you interest**ed** in sports?
l   **I often** play tennis and I sometimes play golf.

B What do you say?

This exercise is a controlled review of the main functional language points from the first four units.

● Introduce the activity by asking learners how they would introduce a colleague to a business partner and write suggestions on the board. They should then look at the sentences in their books and find the appropriate phrase in the second column.

● Alone or in pairs, learners match the remaining functions to the words said.

Answers
1c   2h   3e   4g   5a   6b   7d   8f

● Check their answers and then elicit other suggestions for each function. If necessary, write these on the board.

● In pairs, learners write a short dialogue incorporating **three** of the above phrases. Either let them decide on their own situation or give each pair a different situation.

● Go round helping them while they are doing this. When they have finished, give them time to practise and memorize their dialogue.

● Round up by asking some of the pairs to act out their conversation to the rest of the class.

C Vocabulary

● In pairs or small groups, learners write down as many words as they can for each heading. Set a time limit of two minutes for the first heading and then go through the answers, writing them up on the board. Proceed in the same way with the remaining two headings. To add a competitive element, allow each pair or team to score one point for each correct item (correct spelling included!).

- As consolidation, ask learners to give definitions of some of the words they came up with.

D Reading

- Ask learners to skim through the article and find out what line of business Reuben Singh is in. Then ask them to reread the article and underline anything they find unusual about him. Let them compare their answers with a partner before going on to a class discussion.

- If you wish to go into more detail, divide learners into pairs and ask them to write five questions on the article. Go around checking that their questions are both grammatically correct and appropriate while they are doing this. Then ask them to pass their questions onto another pair for them to answer.

E Listening

- Ask learners if they can imagine what a typical day for Reuben Singh would be like. Then write the times on the board and ask them, in pairs, to suggest what he does at these times.

- Learners listen and compare Christine's day with their own suggestions. The second time they should complete the notes in their books.

    Answers
    5.00   gets up
    7.00   goes to the office and works until 8.30
    8.45   goes to school
    12.30   goes back to the office for an hour
    15.30   finishes school and goes back to the office
    21.00   revises for exams
    24.00   goes to bed

Tapescript

INTERVIEWER: Christine, you're not only a typical eighteen year old, studying for your A levels; you're also a very successful businesswoman. How do you manage to combine these two things? Perhaps you could tell me about a typical day?

CHRISTINE: Sure. Well, I usually get up about five o'clock. I try to get to the office for seven and then design jewellery for an hour and a half until it's time to dash off to school which starts at a quarter to nine.

INTERVIEWER: And then you're at school all day?

CHRISTINE: No, not at all. When the others go off for lunch, I go back to the office for another hour's work.

INTERVIEWER: What time do you finish school?

CHRISTINE: Half past three.

INTERVIEWER: What do you do then?

CHRISTINE: It's back to the office until about nine. This is when people who manufacture jewellery for me bring it in for distribution – I also have to give them new supplies – it's quite chaotic!

INTERVIEWER: So when do you find time to study?

CHRISTINE: After that. I usually do about three hours' revision before I go to bed at midnight.

INTERVIEWER: What are you going to do when you finish school?

CHRISTINE: I plan to do business studies at Birmingham University.

INTERVIEWER: Do you really need to? I mean, you already have a lot of business experience.

CHRISTINE: Er, I expect it'll be a little strange to learn the theory after having been involved in the practical side since I was thirteen. But –

INTERVIEWER: What do your school friends think of this?

CHRISTINE: They've always thought I was a little different. They were interested in music, I was interested in business and politics.

INTERVIEWER: Do you have time for a social life?

CHRISTINE: As I make and sell jewellery, when I do go out, I'm more interested in what people are wearing than enjoying myself. I never turn off!

- To finish off, learners make notes about a typical day in their lives and then compare notes with a partner.

Summary

The summary recapitulates the main language points in each group of units. Ask learners to look through it and find out if they have any questions.

The *Useful words and expressions* section lists the main lexis from each group of units. If your learners all have the same mother tongue, put them into small groups to write their own translations of the items listed. This will probably lead to a fruitful discussion of the translation of more difficult words and phrases. If your learners do not speak the same language, it is probably best left for them to do with a dictionary at home. They could, however, compare the 'List' sections with another learner.

6 Transportation

This unit deals with transport and infrastructure. Learners will practise talking about infrastructure, describing facilities, comparing advantages and disadvantages, and dealing with orders, specifically with the delivery instructions of an order. Comparative and superlative adjectives are reviewed, and adjectives describing quality are practised. There is also practice given in correcting punctuation and capitalization.

Further Ahead Video Sequence 2, 'The Delivery', covers the themes dealt with in Units 6 to 9 of the Learner's Book.

6.1 Describing infrastructure

A Vocabulary

- Learners look at the artwork and name the items in the pictures, using the words to help them.

B Reading

- Learners look at the map and establish where Virginia is. Then give them a couple of minutes to skim through the text and find out how many different forms of transport are mentioned.

    Answer
    Four (air, sea, rail, road)

- Learners read the missing sentences and then reread the text to work out where they belong. You could ask them to underline the items of vocabulary which helped them work this out. With a class that finds reading difficult, ask them to do this before they reread the text.

    Answers
    1c 2a 3d 4e 5b

C Vocabulary

- Write the three headings on the board (+++, +/−, −−−) and elicit any vocabulary that can be used to say how good something is. They then complete the task in their books.

Answers

+++	+/−	−−−
excellent	adequate	poor
very good	satisfactory	terrible
first class	fair	unsatisfactory

- Ask learners to describe transport facilities in your area or their home towns using these words. Prompt them by asking questions such as *Is there an airport near here? What's it like? What are the railway links like?* etc.

D Reading and speaking

- Divide the class into two groups and get them to look at their respective files. In their groups, they should read them through and rate the facilities, underlining key facts while they are doing this. Make sure there is consensus in the groups concerning the ratings.

- Regroup learners so they are working in pairs with a member from the other group. They should then find out about their partner's city. They should not only give the rating while they are doing this, but also reasons for it.

- While they are doing this, go around and listen in to monitor language for feedback afterwards. Finally, round off by asking a few general questions, e.g.: *What is the port like in Sydney? Are there good railway links in Singapore?* etc.

6.2 Forms of transport

Ⓐ Listening and presentation

- Elicit different ways of transporting goods, either drawing on learners' knowledge or by using pictures from magazines etc. and write these as headings on the board, i.e. *air, sea, rail* and *road*.

- In pairs or small groups, give learners a few minutes to brainstorm the advantages (+++) and disadvantages (– – –) of each method of transport. Then collate information under the above headings on the board.

- Learners look at the table in their book and try to decide which method of transport is being referred to.

- Learners listen and compare their answers with the tape.

  ### Answers
  a air/low insurance costs
  b sea/slow
  c road/pollution
  d rail/little pollution

Tapescript

INTERVIEWER:	How do you recommend that your clients send their goods overseas?
MAN:	Well, there's no simple answer to that, it depends on a number of factors. For example, if speed is essential, we recommend air freight. It's faster than any other means of transportation.
INTERVIEWER:	But that's very expensive, isn't it?
MAN:	Sure. But it's better to pay more than to be late delivering the goods. And in one way it isn't expensive at all. Insurance for air freight is cheap, much cheaper than for sea freight.
INTERVIEWER:	So do you ever recommend shipping goods sea freight?
MAN:	Oh, yes. If a client has large quantities or very heavy machinery, it's the only answer. But it's much slower. And port fees and delays can make it just as expensive as air freight.
INTERVIEWER:	What about goods that are transported nationally? Do you recommend truck or rail?
MAN:	Well usually truck because you can deliver direct to the customer. Its advantage over rail is that it isn't dependent on a set route, so it's much more flexible. One problem with road transportation is the pollution factor and this is where rail has a definite advantage. Rail is also more economical in the use of labour. You can transport up to sixty carloads of goods with a small crew.

Ⓑ Grammar

- Write on the board:

  Transporting goods by air … transporting goods by sea.

  and ask learners for suggestions to complete the sentence. If necessary, give prompts such as *fast* and *expensive* and elicit the two ways of comparing adjectives, depending on adjective length.

  … (adjective + er) than …
  … more (adjective) than …

- Then turn the sentence round and ask learners to complete the sentence, this time starting off with *Transporting goods by sea …* to show the other way of making comparisons.

  … not as (adjective) as …

- In pairs, learners make some sentences comparing air and road transport. They should start each sentence with *Transporting goods by air is* to ensure they use both forms of the comparison.

  ### Suggested answers

Transporting goods by air is	not as cheap as faster than more difficult than not as dangerous as not as slow as more expensive than not as easy as safer than	by road.

- Give learners a few minutes to discuss the next point. Encourage them to justify their answers.

Suggested answers

(This will depend to some extent on what is being transported and to where.)

a   Road is the most flexible.
b   Rail (?) is the most reliable.
c   Rail is the most environmentally friendly.

C   Vocabulary

- Learners match the type of cargo to the symbol.

Answers

1c   2e   3a   4b   5d   6f

D   Speaking and writing

- Before starting this exercise, you might review language used to advise or recommend: *I think …, You should …, It would be better to/a good idea to … .* Brainstorm in pairs, then supplement learners' suggestions. Then, go over the first situation together, making sure it is clear by asking questions such as *What is the cargo? What methods of transport could be used?* Ask learners to suggest the pros and cons of each method that comes into question

(road and rail here) before they arrive at a recommendation.

- In small groups, learners discuss the other situations. A secretary should make notes on the pros and cons of each method and the solution to be suggested to the client.

- If you are short of time, each group can present their solutions orally and write them up for homework.

6.3 Dealing with an order

A   Reading and writing

- Learners look at the fax quickly. Ask a few questions orally to check general comprehension, e.g. *Who is the fax to? Who is it from? What did Ms Sanchez order? When will the goods arrive?* etc.

- Elicit when capital letters are used in English. Learners reread the fax and complete the header. Check their answers before asking them to punctuate the body of the fax.

- The corrected fax should look like this:

V A C
Industries

28 Devon Road,
Plymouth
PL1 1HZ

Fax: ++44 (0)1752 323821
Tel: ++44 (0)1752 328822

Attention : <u>Ms Sanchez</u>
Company : <u>Royale Engineering Company</u>
Country : <u>Spain</u>
From   : Brian Davison
Date   : <u>28 August</u>

Dear Ms Sanchez

Thank you for your order of 23 August. We are pleased to confirm your order of 20 units of model 1203, payment by letter of credit. We will deliver the goods by 20 September by ship to Bilbao. I will send you shipping details on Monday.

I look forward to hearing from you soon.

Yours sincerely

Brian Davison
Marketing Manager

Photocopiable © Cambridge University Press 1998

B Listening

- Learners listen to a message on Brian Davison's answering machine from Ms Sanchez.

  Answer
  Method of delivery

📼 💿 *Tapescript*

DAVISON: This is Brian Davison speaking. I'm afraid I'm not in my office at the moment, but if you would like to leave a message, I will return your call as soon as possible.

SANCHEZ: This is Manuela Sanchez from Royale Engineering in San Sebastian, Spain. I'm calling about the delivery conditions for our order for machine spare parts, er, that's order number A 5490, er, we arranged delivery by ship from Southampton to Bilbao, but I'm afraid that something has come up and we now need the consignment rather urgently. Would it be possible for you to send it air freight to San Sebastian as soon as possible? Of course, we will pay any additional costs that arise. Thank you very much.

C Reading

- Learners read the memo and correct any mistakes. You will probably need to replay the listening for this.

  Answer
  (Incorrect information is underlined. Correct information is in brackets.)

MEMO

Change delivery conditions (Royale Engineering Ms Sanchez) – order no. <u>E</u> (A) 5490.

Air freight to <u>Bilbao</u> (San Sebastian) as soon as possible. Ms Sanchez to pay additional freight costs.

D Writing

- Learners read through the sentences and find the ones which can be used to confirm the changes in delivery.

  Answers
  5 and 2

- In pairs, learners draft the fax to Ms Sanchez. It does not need to go much beyond these two sentences, but should nevertheless include details of the order number and destination (see corrected memo above).

  Suggested answer

VAC Industries

28 Devon Road, Plymouth PL1 1HZ

Fax: ++44 (0)1752 323821
Tel: ++44 (0)1752 328822

Attention : Ms Sanchez
Company : Royale Engineering Company
Country : Spain
From : Brian Davison
Date : 30 August

Message

Dear Ms Sanchez

We have arranged for the immediate dispatch of order A 5490 by air freight to San Sebastian. Additional charges for delivery by air freight will be paid by you.

Regards

Photocopiable © Cambridge University Press 1998

7 Imports and exports

Imports and exports has a very international flavour, allowing learners to think about trade in various nations of the world. Types of industry are discussed, and learners review mass and count nouns in the context of imports and exports. The present perfect is introduced and contrasted with the past simple.

7.1 Talking about industries

A Vocabulary

● Write *Mexico* on the board and brainstorm all that learners know about it. Then ask them to look at the maps in their books and the icons of the different industries. Elicit as many names as possible and write them on the board in random order. Learners match them to the icons.

Answers
a Petroleum
b Computers
c Textiles
d Automobile
e Agriculture
f Pharmaceuticals
g Chemical
h Tourism

B Listening

● Ask learners to look at the list again and guess which industries are imports and which ones are exports. They then listen and check their answers.

Answers
Exports: Petroleum, textile, automobile, agriculture, tourism
Imports: Computers, pharmaceuticals, chemicals

 *Tapescript*

MEXICAN: Our main export is petroleum and petroleum products. Many people don't know this, but Mexico has one of the largest oil reserves in the world outside the Middle East. And so it's a very important industry for our country. In fact, it's one of our main employers.

INTERVIEWER: What about hi-tech industries such as the computer industry?

MEXICAN: Well, although we still import most of our needs in this area, a number of American, Japanese and Taiwanese hi-tech companies are now producing their products in Mexico. We expect this sort of cooperation to continue and that Mexican companies will soon start producing their own hi-tech equipment to export to other countries.

In other manufacturing areas we are quite strong. We have a growing textile industry and a thriving automobile industry. Volkswagen, General Motors and Ford all have large plants here and we expect other foreign car manufacturers to relocate too.

INTERVIEWER: What about the pharmaceutical and chemical industries?

MEXICAN: We rely on imports to cover our needs in this area.

INTERVIEWER: And other industries?

MEXICAN: Well, agriculture is important. We produce a lot of fruit and vegetables for the local and North American market. And another developing industry is tourism. We have such beauty and diversity of countryside as well as history and culture that it is easy to understand why Mexico is one of the most

27

popular tourist destinations in the world, and I'm very proud to be part of such an important industry …

C Vocabulary

● Elicit what each type of industry does: commodities – natural products sold at a profit; manufacturing – making a product from raw materials; services – providing a service rather than goods. Then preteach any industries in the box you think will be unfamiliar by giving examples. In pairs, learners categorize them.

Answers

Commodities	Manufacturing	Services
rice	electronic goods	retailing
coffee	pharmaceuticals	banking
wool	furniture	insurance
coal	cars	advertising

● Finally, ask learners to suggest a couple of other industries for each category.

D Speaking

● Learners make notes on important industries in their area. If they are all from the same area, they can do this in pairs or small groups.

7.2 Talking about imports and exports

A Presentation

● Brainstorm what learners know about South Korea, in particular any companies they might know and what they export. Then ask them to look at the pie chart and read the sentences below, deciding which ones are true and which ones are false.

Answers
1F 2T 3F 4T 5F 6T

● See if learners can correct the sentences which were false.

B Grammar

● Make sure learners are aware of the difference between countable and uncountable nouns by letting them categorize the following into countable and uncountable nouns: *coal, textiles, iron, machinery, chemicals, computers, steel, ships, rice, pigs, tobacco.*

● Ask them to look at the diagrams in their books showing the differing expressions of quantity. In pairs, they complete the dialogue. In some instances, there is more than one correct answer, so allow for discussion.

Suggested answers
2 a lot/not much
3 many
4 a lot/not many
5 a lot of/much
6 a little
7 a lot of/many
8 a few

C Writing

● In pairs or small groups, learners write some sentences about the graph. To make the task more of a challenge, set a time limit of ten minutes for the task. To introduce a competitive element, have each team read a sentence and award one point for each correct answer (grammatically and content-wise)!

Suggested answers
1 South Korea exports only a few minerals.
2 South Korea exports a lot of chemicals.
3 South Korea exports a lot of textiles.
4 South Korea exports quite a lot of iron and metals.
5 South Korea doesn't export much machinery.
6 South Korea doesn't export many electrical products.

D Speaking

● Divide learners into two groups and ask them to look at their respective file cards. First of all, they should make some sentences about their pie charts and then prepare questions to ask about their partner's chart.

● Give them a few minutes' preparation time and then regroup learners into pairs to exchange information on their countries. Listen in and make a note of good and bad use of language to give feedback on when the activity is finished.

7.3 Made in America

(A) Discussion and reading

- Introduce the topic by writing *Made in America* on the board and asking learners for their ideas on this, i.e. whether this is a sign of quality for them, if they like to buy American goods, etc. Find out what they know about American manufacturing – product development (e.g. Is American industry innovative?), production methods (e.g. What role does quality play?), relations in American firms (e.g. Are workers well-treated, 'hire and fire', etc.) – and then ask them to look at the statements in their books. Point out that these refer to the state of American manufacturing in the **1980s** and not now! Individually learners mark whether they are true or false (without referring to the text below!). If they have no opinion on a particular statement, they should mark it with *?*.

- Give learners a few minutes to read through the article and find out if their opinions are correct. They can mark the relevant bits of text as they are reading.

- Let them compare their ideas with a partner before going through the answers with the class.

  Answers
  1F 2T 3T 4F 5T 6T

(B) Reading

- Learners read through the article and match each paragraph to a paragraph in the previous article. Encourage them to justify their choices and underline vocabulary which helped them.

  Answers
  1c 2e 3f 4a 5d 6b

- As an optional activity, ask learners to look at the two texts and tell you what tenses they are written in and why. (The first one uses the past simple; it's talking about a finished period of time. The second one uses the present perfect and present progressive; it deals with change and the current situation.)

(C) Grammar

- Establish that when we are talking about a definite time in the past, we use the past simple; when the time factor is not so important and we are thinking more about the results now we use the present perfect.

- Individually or in pairs, learners complete the grammar exercise. Encourage them to justify their answers.

  Answers
  1 employed
  2 has invested
  3 has consolidated
  4 has sold
  5 lost
  6 went up

(D) Speaking

- If your learners all work in the same company, start off by getting them to think of an area they all know about such as language training. Ask them to think about the situation ten years ago (five will probably be more appropriate if your learners are young!) and write key words on the board. Then ask them to think about what has changed since then.

- If your learners come from different companies or are pre-work, build up examples using local industry, e.g. new industrial parks, companies which have opened up, closed down, etc.

- In pairs or small groups, learners note ten things which have changed in their area or company. Give them a limit of five minutes for this and then ask them to compare their lists with another learner. To encourage discussion, get learners to agree on the 'best' and the 'worst' change.

8 Arrangements

Arrangements deals with planning for business trips and making appointments for business meetings. Learners will have the opportunity to practise talking about schedules, making and changing arrangements and appointments, dealing with correspondence related to travel, and making a telephone call to arrange a meeting. Future time is dealt with, and present progressive for arrangements and the *will* future for spontaneous offers is introduced.

8.1 Discussing an itinerary

A Warmer

- Find out if learners go on business trips themselves or if they are involved in preparing them for other people. Brainstorm the types of arrangements that have to be made for a business trip in the learners' own country, e.g. booking accommodation, arranging appointments, etc. and for a business trip to another country, e.g. booking flights, arranging visas, ordering travellers' cheques, etc.

B Listening and presentation

- Tell learners they will be listening to a businesswoman discussing her schedule with her secretary for a trip to Bombay and see if there is anything they wish to add or delete from their list. They can use this for a first listening task.

- The second time they listen, learners should complete the itinerary. This is the completed itinerary:

🔲 ◎ *Tapescript*

OLIVIA:	Let's just go over the arrangements for my trip to Bombay.
ASSISTANT:	Sure, here's your schedule. You're flying at 9.55 on Monday evening. That's British Airways flight 139. Er, you have to check in two hours before so I've arranged for a car to pick you up from the office at 6.30.
OLIVIA:	Good. What time does the flight get into Bombay?
ASSISTANT:	It gets into Bombay at 11.15 p.m. That's local time, of course. Er, I've booked you a room at the Oberoi. They're sending a car to pick you up.
OLIVIA:	Fine. Now when am I seeing Mr Shah?
ASSISTANT:	Tuesday afternoon at two. By the way, Mr Majundar is coming to the meeting as well.

Olivia Miller – Trip to Bombay

Monday, October 3rd

6.30 p.m.	Car to London Heathrow, Terminal 4
9.55 p.m.	BA Flight 139 to Bombay
11.15 p.m.	Arrive Bombay, transfer to hotel

Tuesday, October 4th

| 2 p.m. | Meeting with Mr Shah |

Wednesday, October 5th

| All day | Tour of new plant in Bombay and meeting with directors |

Thursday, October 6th

1.15 a.m.	BA flight 138 to London Heathrow
6.25 a.m.	Arrive London Heathrow
3 p.m.	Sales meeting, London

Photocopiable © Cambridge University Press 1998

OLIVIA: That's good news, we won't have to arrange a separate meeting. And has the tour of the new plant in Bombay and the meeting with the directors been arranged for Wednesday?

ASSISTANT: Yes, they'll pick you up in the morning at 9, and plan to show you the plant, take you to lunch, and return you to the hotel at about 5 p.m.

OLIVIA: Good. Now, has my visa arrived?

ASSISTANT: No, not yet. I'll phone the embassy and find out if they've sent it off yet.

OLIVIA: Thanks. And could you order some travellers' cheques?

ASSISTANT: Sure, I'll phone the bank.

OLIVIA: And when am I flying back?

ASSISTANT: I'm afraid the earliest flight I could get is Thursday at 1.15 a.m., everything else was booked up. That's British Airways again, flight 138. That gets you back into London at 6.25 Thursday morning. You've got Thursday in London for the Sales Meeting, but not until 3 p.m., then Friday morning you're leaving for New York …

C Grammar

- See if learners can remember how the assistant talked about the arrangements for the flight and the meeting with Mr Shah. Write on the board:

| *You're* | *flying on Monday evening.* |
| | *seeing Mr Shah on Tuesday.* |

- Then see if they can remember what she said about the visa and travellers' cheques. Elicit and write on the board:

| *I'll* | *phone the embassy.* |
| | *order some travellers' cheques.* |

- Establish that both tenses are used to talk about the future. Try and elicit the difference between them, i.e. the present progressive is used to talk about something which has already been arranged, whereas the *will* future is used for a decision made at the moment of speaking.

- In pairs, learners complete the dialogue. They can check their answers in pairs and then practise it.

Answers
1 When *am I flying* to New York?
2 Where *am I staying*?
3 When *am I seeing* Bill Urwin?
4 *Is Neil coming* to the meeting too?
5 *I'll fax* it this afternoon.

D Speaking

- Divide learners into two groups and ask them to look at their respective file cards. Give them a few minutes to prepare what they want to say and then regroup learners into pairs.

- Ask learners to sit back to back while they are making their phone call. Listen in and make a note of good and bad use of language to give feedback on when the activity is finished.

8.2 Dealing with correspondence

A Reading and presentation

The focus of this section is on correspondence that may arise in connection with a business trip.

- Begin by asking learners to imagine they are going on a three-day business trip at the end of next month and think about the kind of letters and faxes they might have to write in this connection, e.g. booking accommodation, arranging meetings, making, accepting or declining invitations, etc.

- Make sure they understand the functions in the task by giving examples if necessary. Then give learners about five minutes to read through the letters and match each letter to a function.

Answers
1d 2a 3f 4c 5b 6e

- Learners reread the letters and underline words and expressions that helped them identify the type of letter.

B Language focus

- Write the headings from the language box on the board:
  Requesting
  Giving good news
  Giving bad news
  Thanking
  Confirming

and ask learners to find examples of these functions in the letters. They can then compare their answers with the language box before going on to rewrite the instructions to make them more polite.

Suggested answers

1 I would be grateful if you could cancel my reservation.
2 We are pleased to inform you that Mr Petersen will attend the reception on 1 May.
3 Unfortunately, Mrs Lindgren cannot attend the reception on 1 May.
4 Would it be possible to have an appointment on 22 May?
5 Would you please send me confirmation of my booking.
6 Thank you very much for dinner last week.

Ⓒ Listening

● This listening provides a basis for the letter writing in the next section. Learners listen to extract from a conversation.

Answers

1b   2c   3c

🔊 *Tapescript*

JEFF:	I've just been on the phone to HQ. They're having problems with their new software so I'm going to have to go down to Orlando next week.
ASSISTANT:	Do you want to stay at the Marriot?
JEFF:	Yes. You'd better book me a room for three nights. From the 19th to the 21st.
ASSISTANT:	Right. There's one slight problem. The meeting with Mr Wong at Orion is on the 21st. Should I cancel it?
JEFF:	Yes. Maybe you can suggest a new date. Or no, tell him I'll get in touch with him when I get back …

Ⓓ Writing

● In pairs, learners draft a fax to the Marriot, booking accommodation from 19 to 21 January and a fax to Mr Wong at Orion cancelling the meeting on 21 January.

● They should use the letters on the previous page as a model; if necessary ask them to refer to Unit 6 for the layout of a fax.

● In class it is probably sufficient to ask them to write one fax. Either let them choose which one they wish to write or, with a larger class, assign pairs a letter to write. They can then pass them round for other learners to read once they have finished.

Suggested answers

Attention:	**Marriot Hotel, Orlando**
From:	**Jeff Morgan**
Date:	**14 January**

Dear Sir or Madam:

Please could you reserve a single room with shower for the nights of 19, 20 and 21 January.

I would be grateful if you could confirm my reservation by fax.

Regards,

Jeff Morgan

Photocopiable © Cambridge University Press 1998

Attention:	**Mr Wong**
Company:	**Orion**
From:	**Jeff Morgan**
Date:	**14 January**

Dear Mr Wong:

I'm afraid I will have to cancel our meeting on 21 January.

Please accept my apologies. I will contact you as soon as I return to arrange another date.

Regards,

Jeff Morgan

Photocopiable © Cambridge University Press 1998

8.3 Making and changing an appointment

A Listening and presentation

● Play the first phone call and ask learners to note who the meeting is with and when.

Answer
Ian Norman on Monday at 10.00

● Proceed in the same way with the second phone call.

Answer
Mr Matthews on Monday at 11.00

● The completed diary now looks like this:

	October
_10.00_ Ian	MON. **10**
_11.00_ Mr Matthews	
	TUE. **11**
Present new brochures	WED. **12**
_2.30_ Mr. Bloch	THUR. **13**
_9.0_ Printer's	FRI. **14**
	SAT. **15**
	SUN. **16**

Photocopiable © Cambridge University Press 1998

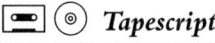 ***Tapescript***

Call one

IAN: Ian Norman speaking.
KATE: Hello Ian, this is Kate. How are you?
IAN: Fine, fine. And yourself?
KATE: A bit stressed with the new catalogue at the moment. It's got to be at the printers by the end of the month. Actually, that's the reason I'm ringing you. Can we fix a time to discuss it?

IAN: Sure. When would be convenient?
KATE: Well, are you free next Monday?
IAN: Yes, as far as I know. I'll just check my diary. Er, what time?
KATE: Early morning would suit me best. Shall we say ten o'clock? In my office?
IAN: Er, yes, that's fine.
KATE: Right. Then I'll see you on Monday at ten.

Call two

KATE: Kate Williams.
SECRETARY: Good morning. This is Brian Matthew's secretary. Mr Matthews will be in Bristol on Monday and he'd like to see you to discuss the marketing plan for next spring. Can we fix a time?
KATE: Sure. When would suit him best?
SECRETARY: Well, he's got quite a full schedule already. Would eleven o'clock be OK?
KATE: I'll just have a look. I've actually got a meeting then. But I can try and change it.
SECRETARY: That would be a great help.
KATE: I'll get back to you in a minute.
SECRETARY: Thanks very much.

B Language focus

● See if learners can remember any of the expressions the speakers used to make the two appointments. Then ask them to look at the cues in the guided dialogue and go through it as a whole class, eliciting suggestions for each line.

● Drill these line by line and then run through the whole dialogue with a learner yourself. Learners practise in open and then closed pairs until they feel confident.

● Finally, write up a model dialogue with alternatives on the board.

C Listening and presentation

● Elicit suggestions as to what Kate Williams will now say to Ian Norman when she calls him again. They then listen and note the new time of the meeting.

Answer
Monday at nine fifteen.

- Ask them to listen a second time for the way Kate asked Ian to change the appointment and write useful expressions on the board, e.g. *Something's come up. Could we meet a little earlier?*

Tapescript

IAN: This is Ian Norman speaking. Please leave a message after the signal.

KATE: Hello, Ian. This is Kate again. The reason I'm calling is that something's come up, I have to see Brian Matthews from Head Office at eleven on Monday. Could we meet a little earlier, say nine fifteen? Could you give me a ring to confirm it? Thanks very much.

D Speaking

- Divide learners into two groups and ask them to look at their respective file cards. Give them a few minutes to prepare what they want to say and then regroup learners into pairs.

- Ask learners to sit back to back while they are making their phone call. Listen in and make a note of good and bad use of language to give feedback on when the activity is finished.

9 Products and services

This unit, which takes products and services as its theme, presents and practises language used in describing a product, making and dealing with complaints, and apologizing. Adjectives describing materials, shapes and colours are introduced and practised.

9.1 Services

Ⓐ Reading

The topic of this section is personal banking.

- Begin by eliciting from learners what they use a bank for and write suggestions on the board, e.g.: *to deposit money, to withdraw cash, to pay bills, to borrow money, to obtain foreign currency, to get investment advice.* This will give you an opportunity to preteach some of the items that come up in the reading.

- Tell learners they are going to read a leaflet about a new type of bank. Set a limit of about five minutes for the reading.

  Answers
  Services include: 24 hours a day home banking, helpful representatives, good interest rates, bill payment facility, foreign money and travellers' cheques, up to £500 a day from cash machines, £100 cheque guarantee.

- Then ask learners to reread the leaflet to correct the statements in their books. They can do this individually or in pairs.

  Answers
  a   First Direct has *no branches*.
  b   The bank is open *24 hours a day, seven days a week.*
  c   *Interest rates* are higher than in other banks.
  d   It offers a *full* range of services.
  e   You can withdraw £500 a *day* from cash machines in the UK.
  f   You can guarantee cheques up to *£100*.

Ⓑ Vocabulary

- Learners reread to find the definitions.

  Answers
  a   to set foot inside   d   representative
  b   branch   e   interest rates
  c   division   f   overheads

Ⓒ Listening

- Learners listen to a potential customer phoning First Direct and note down the questions he asks.

  Answers
  1   How can he pay money into his account?
  2   Does the bank pay interest on his current account?

- Ask learners to listen again and give you feedback on the call, i.e. do they find the person at the bank friendly, helpful, etc. Draw their attention to things which aid this impression such as intonation, using the customer's name, offering information, the way the call is begun and ended, etc.

🔊 *Tapescript*

FIRST DIRECT: Hello, this is First Direct, how can I help you?

MAN: This is Ahmed Aziz speaking. Er, I'm interested in opening an account with you, but I have a couple of questions.

FIRST DIRECT: What exactly would you like to know, Mr Aziz?

MAN: First of all, if I bank with you, how do I pay money into my account?

FIRST DIRECT: Well, as you probably know, First Direct is a part of the Midland Bank. That means you can pay into your First Direct account at any of their branches.

MAN: I see. Er, do they charge me for that?

FIRST DIRECT: No, that's free.

MAN: OK. Right. The other thing I wanted to know was do you pay interest on current accounts?

FIRST DIRECT: Yes, we do. As long as your account is in credit. The interest is then calculated

35

daily, and we add it to your account at the end of each month.

MAN: Uh uh.

FIRST DIRECT: Is there anything else you'd like to know, Mr Aziz?

MAN: No, I think that's all for the time being. Thank you. Goodbye.

FIRST DIRECT: Thank you for calling, Mr Aziz. Goodbye.

D Speaking

- Find out how learners rate the banking staff they deal with, i.e. do they find them friendly and efficient. Establish criteria for meeting this, e.g. they greet the customers, smile, ask if there is anything else they can do at the end of a transaction, etc. Speed of service might also be a criterion.

- Divide learners into two groups and ask them to look at their respective file cards. Give them a few minutes to prepare what they want to say and then regroup into pairs.

- Ask learners to sit back to back while they are making their phone call. Listen in and note use of language to give feedback on when the activity is finished. Alternatively, put two pairs together if you have a large class or, with a smaller class, ask a pair to act out their role play for the other members. You could ask listeners to award points from a scale of 1–10 (1 = unfriendly, unhelpful, inefficient, 10 = friendly, helpful and efficient) and encourage comments from other learners.

9.2 Describing a product

A Warmer

- Ask learners to look at the bed or draw a sketch of it on the board. Establish *length, width, depth* and *height*. Then elicit questions learners can ask to find out the missing information, e.g. *How long is it? How high is it? What colours is it available in? What's it made of?* etc.

- Draw attention to the nouns and adjectives:

height	high
length	long
width	wide
depth	deep
weight	How much does it weigh? (with verb)

- Ask learners to imagine they are interested in buying this product and if there are any other things they would like to know, e.g. delivery times, guarantee, etc.

B Listening and presentation

- Learners listen and complete the missing information.

Answers

Length:	204 cm
Width:	101.5 cm
Height:	172 cm
Colours:	natural, red and turquoise
Material:	wood
Price:	$399

Tapescript

SALES REP: Right. Now this range of children's furniture is ideal from toddlers all the way through to teenagers. As you know, a child's needs change quite quickly in the first few years of their life so you need something that is flexible. Here you can start off with one or two basic items and then add more as the child gets older, a wardrobe, more shelves, perhaps a desk once they start school.

Now let me start by showing you the bed. Would you like to come over here? Now this is a standard size single bed.

CUSTOMER: How long is it? We don't have a lot of space, so every centimeter counts.

SALES REP: Outside measurements are 204 cm by 101.5 cm.

CUSTOMER: Uh uh. That should fit. And how high is it? It looks quite high.

SALES REP: 172 cm. So you can have a play area underneath or, if necessary, add a second bed. It's made of solid wood and comes in a natural wood finish as you see it here. It's also available with turquoise and red applications.

CUSTOMER: It looks very nice. How much does it cost?

SALES REP: The basic bed as you see it here is $399.

CUSTOMER: I see. And what about delivery times?

SALES REP: About six weeks from date of order.

CUSTOMER: Do we have to pick it up?
SALES REP: No, no, we deliver anywhere within Metro Toronto, and …

C **Vocabulary**

- Draw some of the shapes on the board if you think learners will be unfamiliar with them and show objects made of various materials to preteach some of the vocabulary in this task. Ask questions such as *What shape is it? What's it made of?*

- Then ask learners to look at the vocabulary in their books and put it into categories.

  Answers

Shape	Fabric	Quality
square	metal	easy-to-use
sphere	wood	good-value
cube	leather	flexible
cone	cotton	attractive
triangle	wool	

- Describe something you have in your pocket or bag and have learners guess what it is. Put learners into small groups and let them take it in turns to describe objects they have on them. Alternatively, make it into a competition by dividing the class into two teams.

D **Speaking**

- Start off by asking learners to look at the cartoon and describe the machine. Then build up a profile of it together, using the language in their books.

- Divide learners into two groups and ask them to look at their respective file cards. Let them prepare their description in small groups. Give them a few minutes to do this, and then regroup learners into pairs to sell their product to their partner.

9.3 Keeping the customer happy

A **Listening and presentation**

- Introduce the topic by asking learners how you can keep customers happy. If they are in work, they should draw on their experience there; if they are pre-work, ask them to think of situations they have found themselves in and been either extremely satisfied or, conversely, dissatisfied with the service provided.

- Learners listen to the first phone call and find out what the problem is.

Answer
Ms Austin is still waiting for some brochures from the printer.

- Learners then listen to the second phone call and answer the questions in their books.

  Answers
  1 A90 range.
  2 By Friday.

Tapescript

First call
PRINTER: Phoenix Printers. Good morning.
AUSTIN: This is Jennifer Austin from Leroy Motors. Could I speak to Leo Dayton, please?
PRINTER: I'm afraid he's not in at the moment. Can I give him a message?
AUSTIN: Well, I'm ringing about a reprint of one of our brochures. I asked him to do it six weeks ago and we're still waiting for them. If I remember rightly, I did say it was rather urgent.
PRINTER: I'll get him to call you back as soon as he comes in, Ms Austin.
AUSTIN: Thank you very much.

Second call
AUSTIN: This is Jennifer Austin speaking.
DAYTON: Leo Dayton from Phoenix Printers. I understand there's been a problem with an order.
AUSTIN: That's right. I asked you to do a reprint of our A90 brochure some time ago and we still don't have it.
DAYTON: Yes. I've just been trying to find out what happened. It seems some urgent work came in and your order got overlooked. I'm really sorry.
AUSTIN: I see. Well, the problem is we have an exhibition coming up at the beginning of next month and we'll want to have them for then. How soon can you get them done?
DAYTON: Would the end of the week be OK?
AUSTIN: That'd be great.
DAYTON Right, then. I'll see that you get them by Friday. And I'm really sorry about this.
AUSTIN: Don't worry.

B Reading

● Set the situation by explaining that customers have been asking for information on the A90 range of motors. Ask learners what they would do if there were no brochures available. If necessary, point out that not doing anything will not create a very good impression with customers!

● With a stronger group try and elicit suggestions for a possible letter to customers. Then get them to compare their ideas with the letter in their book. Otherwise ask learners to read through the letter and find out why it has been written.

Answers
To apologize for not sending the brochures earlier.
To send them now.

● Ask learners to reread the letter and <u>underline</u> the phrases used to apologize.

Answers
I apologize for the delay in sending you …
Please accept my apologies.

● Write these on the board and contrast them with the spoken language in the next section.

C Language focus

● Ask learners if they can remember how the printer apologized in the phone call in **A**. Elicit any other expressions they can think of and then ask them to look at the guided dialogue in their books.

● Go through it, eliciting and drilling exponents line by line. Then practise the whole dialogue with one learner. Divide learners into pairs and let them practise both roles until they feel confident.

● If necessary, write a model with exponents on the board, as at the top of the next column.

D Speaking

● Learners listen to the voice-mails and then try to resolve the problems. Play them through first to determine what the problems are.

Answers
1 You forget an appointment.
2 Customer hasn't received operating instructions with the consignment.
3 Customer is waiting for you to return call about faulty motors.

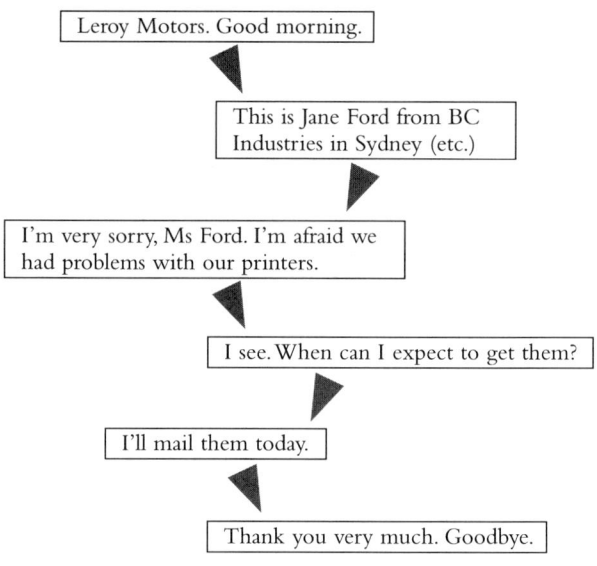

Leroy Motors. Good morning.

This is Jane Ford from BC Industries in Sydney (etc.)

I'm very sorry, Ms Ford. I'm afraid we had problems with our printers.

I see. When can I expect to get them?

I'll mail them today.

Thank you very much. Goodbye.

● Discuss with learners whether they find it more appropriate to write or call in the first situation. (Here it would be more appropriate to call.) Now ask learners to look at the other two situations.

● Divide the class up into pairs or small groups and assign each one a problem. You could set any letters for homework and ask learners to role play the phone calls.

 *Tapescript*

Message one
Hello. This is Anne Wallace. Er, we had a meeting yesterday afternoon at three. Did you forget? Please give me a call so we can arrange a new time. Thank you.

Message two
Hello. This is Max van der Valk from Gamma International in Holland. We've just accepted delivery of a consignment of A45 motors. Unfortunately, there were no operating instructions included. Could you send us them as soon as possible? Thanks.

Message three
Hello. This is Arturo Hernandez from Enigma Engineering. I'm still waiting for you to return my call about the problems we're having with the C60 motors. I thought you were going to ring last week. Please call me as soon as possible. I'll be in my office today until three.

10 Revision and consolidation

A Grammar

This exercise reviews the main grammar points in Units 6 to 10.

● Give learners about 10 to 15 minutes to work through the sentences, correcting the mistakes. It is probably best if they do this in twos or threes as it will encourage discussion of the mistakes and how they should be corrected.

● Then go through the sentences together, establishing what is wrong and how the mistakes can be corrected.

Answers

a Is it quick**er** to transport goods by rail or by road?
b Which is the **most** expensive method of transport?
c We import **a lot of** computers but we don't import much machinery.
d How **many** cars do you export each year?
e Unemployment ~~has~~ increased during the eighties.
f Transport **has** improved a lot. We now have a new rail link.
g When **are you going** to headquarters?
h How **many** nights do you want to stay?
i **I'll book** a room for you at the Sheraton.
j I'm afraid Mr Honda can't come to the meeting because he**'s going** on a course on Thursday.
k How much **do** those shelves over there **weigh**?
l It's 3.5 metres **long**.

B What do you say?

This exercise is a controlled review of the main functional language points from Units 6 to 10.

● Introduce the activity by asking learners how they would describe facilities such as transportation for local industry and write suggestions on the board. They should then look at the sentences in their books and find the appropriate phrase in the second column.

● Alone or in pairs, learners match the remaining functions to the words said.

Answers

1f 2d 3h 4b 5a 6g 7e 8c

● Check learners' answers and then elicit other suggestions for each function. If necessary, write these on the board.

● In pairs, learners write a short dialogue incorporating **three** of the above phrases. Either let them decide on their own situation or give each pair a different situation.

● Go round helping them while they are doing this. When they have finished, give them time to practise and memorize their dialogue. Round up by asking some of the pairs to act out their conversation to the rest of the class.

C Vocabulary

● In pairs or small groups learners categorize the words and find a suitable heading.

Suggested answers

Transportation	Industries	Materials
tanker	oil	plastic
truck	chemicals	leather
port	tourism	wood
container	insurance	cotton

● Ask learners to add a few more words to each category. To round off, ask them to use some of the words in a sentence.

D Listening

● Introduce the topic by asking learners if they are satisfied with their bank and the service it gives. List possible reasons for complaints on the board and ask learners to rank them in order of severity. Then ask learners to compare them with the chart in their books.

● Learners listen and note the reasons Shaw gives for switching banks.

Answers
In the chart:
    Excessive account charges
    Inconvenient branch location
Other reasons:
    Limited overdraft
    Manager unpleasant and unsympathetic after the theft of a credit card

🔊 ◎ *Tapescript*

INTERVIEWER: Mr Shaw, you recently changed banks. Can you tell us something about that?

SHAW: Certainly.

INTERVIEWER: How long were you with your old bank?

SHAW: Five years.

INTERVIEWER: And why did you decide to change?

SHAW: Well, I'm self-employed, I work as a financial adviser and my income varies from month to month. So I need an overdraft facility to cope with this. At my old bank, the overdraft facility was limited and then, when I compared the charges with the rates of my new bank, I realized I was paying far too much. Er, I might have stayed with my old bank, but then a credit card was stolen. The manager who handled the incident was unpleasant and unsympathetic. I think he forgot that I was the customer. And so I decided to change.

INTERVIEWER: Are you satisfied with your new bank?

SHAW: So far, yes. I now pay less for my overdraft and so far, I've found my new bank very helpful. It's also very convenient for me because there is a branch close by and plenty of cash points.

INTERVIEWER: So you don't regret the move?

SHAW: No. And although it seems complicated at first, I'd certainly recommend switching banks if you're not happy with your present one.

E Reading

● Recap the services offered by a bank. Then ask learners what procedures they imagine are involved in switching banks. Let them look at the list in their books and check they understand them. In pairs, they try to put them in order (without referring to the article!). Then give them five minutes to read the article and check the order they chose.

Answers
5 Cut your cheque-guarantee card in half.

3 Tell the new bank to take over payment of the standing orders and direct debits.

6 Write a letter to the old bank to close the account.

1 Instruct your employer to pay your salary into the new account.

2 Ask your old bank to send you a list of standing-order and direct-debit commitments.

4 Cancel the payment of standing orders with the old bank.

Summary

See notes on page 22.

11 Marketing

Marketing gives learners a chance to think about and discuss company image, the different ways of promoting a product, and the advantages and disadvantages of various forms of promotion. Task-based exercises include devising a promotional campaign for a product and choosing and ordering promotional items within a budget for a store opening. Relative pronouns *who* and *which* are practised.

> *Further Ahead* Video Sequence 3, 'What's in a brand name?', covers the themes dealt with in Units 11 to 14 of the Learner's Book.

11.1 Projecting an image

A Warmer

- If you wish, introduce the topic by bringing a variety of local logos to the class and asking the class what they feel about them and what kind of image they think the company is trying to project with them, e.g. *up-market*, *'green'*, *trendy*, etc.

- Ask learners what they know about the British Broadcasting Corporation (the BBC, Britain's state-financed television and radio network). Find out from them if they listen to the BBC's global radio service, the World Service, or know of it. (If learners are interested in listening to it, information about World Service frequencies should be obtainable through the local offices of the British Council.)

- Ask learners to look at the two BBC logos and decide which one they prefer, think is more modern, etc. Try to get them to justify their choices, for example, by explaining why they think it is more modern, up-market, etc. The lower one is the new logo introduced in October 1997.

B Listening

- Make sure learners understand the questions before they listen!

  Answers
  1 It was about to launch a new range of channels and services.

2 It didn't work on screen. It was too expensive to use. There were too many sub-logos.
3 To simplify the logo. To use it as a unifying symbol across all departments and services.
4 £1.7 million.

Tapescript

INTERVIEWER: The British Broadcasting Corporation recently changed its logo. Can you tell us why?

BBC: Well, we were planning the launch of a range of new channels and services at the time, so it was an opportunity for us to think over the existing logo.

INTERVIEWER: You weren't happy with it?

BBC: Basically no. There were a number of problems. For example, it didn't work as an on-screen graphic. Because it sat at an angle, it often appeared to vibrate and the colours disappeared. Then, being four-colour, it was expensive to use. And finally, we felt the BBC had become visually fragmented over the years. By that I mean we had too many sub-logos which weakened the effect of the main brand. With the new logo, the 'BBC' is much stronger and emphasizes the brand.

INTERVIEWER:	So what were your main aims in changing the logo?
BBC:	They were twofold. First, to simplify the design of the logo. Second, to use it as a unifying symbol across all BBC departments and services.
INTERVIEWER:	And do you think the new logo has been a success?
BBC:	I'd say yes. As I said, we wanted something that was simple to use and this logo works well in all media. And I think the design manages to reflect our core values of quality, accuracy and artistic excellence in an increasingly international and competitive news market. So yes, I think it has been a success.
INTERVIEWER:	What about the costs?
BBC:	So far, it's cost us about £1.7 million. Now that may seem a lot of money, but in the long term it will actually save us money because, for example, we will save on print costs by not having to use four colours each time the logo is used.

C Vocabulary

● If you have access to any of these items as realia, bring them to your class. Alternatively, ask learners to look at the artwork in their books and see how many items they can name.

Answers

1	newsletter	6	key ring
2	phone pad	7	baseball cap
3	business card	8	company report
4	letterhead	9	envelope
5	compliments slip	10	pen

D Language focus

● Write on the board:

An invoice is something <u>which</u> …
A customer is someone <u>who</u> …

and ask for suggestions to complete the two sentences. Establish that *who* is used for people and *which* is used for objects. In pairs, learners match a word from the left-hand column with a definition from the right-hand column.

Answers

1 A catalogue is something which lists items for sale and their prices.
2 A newsletter is something which gives news about a company.
3 A supplier is someone who provides a company with goods or equipment.
4 A letterhead is something which is printed at the top of writing paper.
5 A graphic designer is someone who designs logos, etc.
6 A logo is something which is used on products and advertising material.
7 A printer is someone who prints books and leaflets.

● If you have time, ask learners to write a couple of their own definitions for some of the other items in **C**. Alternatively, use the following Resource activity.

Resource activity 5: Definitions

● Photocopy the cards at Resource activity 5 (page 83) and cut them up. Split the class into two teams. Put the cards in a pile and ask Team A to take a card. Give them a couple of minutes to decide how to define the word. Team B then has to guess what the object is. Then Team B proceeds in the same way.

● Score as follows: 3 points for guessing correctly the first time, 2 points the second time and 1 point the third time. The first team to get ten points is the winner.

11.2 Choosing your media

A Warmer

● Ask learners to look at the two products. To introduce some of the vocabulary for the reading below, brainstorm the different ways in which they are advertised and write up suggestions on the board. You could also discuss why different media are used and who they are designed to reach.

Suggested answers

American Express
Advertising in newspapers and magazines, on TV and radio, etc.
Newspaper and magazine inserts
Direct mailing

Levi's
Advertising in magazines and newspapers, on TV and radio, in the cinema, on billboards, etc.

- You could extend this by asking learners how other products such as soft drinks and cars are advertised. With learners who are in work, go on to talk about how their products or services are advertised.

- If you have any realia of your own, such as direct mailing, vouchers, pens with brand names, etc., bring them along to class.

B Reading

- Ask learners to look at the terms in the box and make sure they understand what they mean. (You should have established a few examples of each in the previous discussion.)

- Give them five minutes to read through the article and fill the gaps in each paragraph. When they have finished, ask them to check their answers with a partner.

    Answers
    1   Consumer promotions
    2   Merchandising
    3   Direct mail
    4   Advertising

- Check their answers and then deal with any vocabulary they found difficult.

C Reading

- Learners reread the article and answer the T/F questions.

    Answers
    1T
    2F   They are forms of consumer promotions.
    3T
    4F   It can be extremely cost effective.
    5T
    6F   They are best suited for consumer products.

D Discussion

- Ask learners to look at the first picture (Night Owl coffee) and tell them it is a new brand of decaffeinated coffee which the manufacturer wishes to promote in their country / the country they are learning English in. Ask them to think about the type of people who might buy this coffee and also where it can be bought, e.g. supermarkets, corner shops, mail order, etc. Having established this, elicit ways it could be promoted – and perhaps also ways which would not be successful. For example, in some countries, money-off

vouchers are considered tacky and would dissuade potential customers from trying the product.

- In groups, learners do the same for the other products. When they have finished, ask them to present their findings to the class. If time is short, do one together as a class and give learners the choice of the remaining two to do as a homework assignment.

11.3 Choosing a promotional product for your company

- Start by asking learners how their company promotes their products, e.g. do they use give-aways? Also think about the type of things they might give customers and clients at Christmas and other times of year.

- If your learners are not in work, ask them what kind of give-aways they have received and how they feel about them, for example, do they like to receive such gifts; how does it make them feel about the company which is giving them away.

A Listening

- Make sure learners have the following information:

    Answers
    Promotional gifts for: *all customers*
    No. of items: *5,000*
    Budget: *£2,500*
    Other: *all gifts to have Niche Wear embossed on them*

Tapescript

Right. Now, about this new store we're opening. We've decided that on the day it opens, each customer who buys something in the store will receive a promotional gift. I think we can expect a good turnout on the first day. We'll be advertising in the local press the week beforehand and on billboards, and on local radio. We've allocated a budget of £2,500 for this promotional opening, and what I'd like you to do is to find a suitable gift. Or, er, gifts, I don't think it necessarily has to be the same for everyone. I think we can expect a lot of young mothers, and also a lot of teenagers and I think you should aim for about 5,000 items.

Now the one thing that is important is that the promotional items should have our name embossed on them. If you have any questions, I'll be back in the office at the beginning of next week.

B **Reading and discussion**

● Learners scan this extract from a catalogue and decide upon promotional products. They should do this in pairs or small groups. Encourage them to justify not only their choices, but also their reasons for rejecting items as being unsuitable.

● If you have time, or for homework, learners should write a short report for their boss. Alternatively, ask them to present their findings to another group.

C **Writing**

● Learners complete the order form for the gift(s) they have chosen.

D **Writing**

● First learners look at the phrases in their books and match them up. Then ask them to suggest a sequence for them. Finally, in pairs, they draft the letter, filling in their details with their own information.

● When they have finished, ask learners to show their letter to another pair and to ask for comments.

Model answer
See below.

● As an extension, learners from different groups phone through their order to members of another group, who should note the details on a piece of paper.

Dear Sir or Madam

We would like to place an order for the following items:

1,000 reflectors: *bear* – green
1,000 reflectors: *bear* – blue
1,000 reflectors: *bear* – orange

We enclose your official order form.

Please confirm that you can deliver the goods within 14 days.

We look forward to receiving the goods.

Yours faithfully

Photocopiable © Cambridge University Press 1998

12 Statistics

Statistics introduces learners to language used to describe trends, to talk about cause and effect, and to describe changes in a company's performance. Learners will also discuss a company's training programme and will make a short presentation as part of a task-based exercise. Adjectives and adverbs are revised and practised, and sequencing language to give structure to a presentation is also presented.

12.1 Describing performance

A Reading and presentation

- Draw the three bar charts on the board and see if learners can describe the basic movement using any vocabulary they might already know, e.g. *sales went up/down a lot/ a little*, etc.

- Learners read the three texts and match them with the graphs in their books.

  Answers
  1c 2a 3b

- In pairs, learners reread the texts and underline all the vocabulary which describes an upward or downward movement.

  Text 1
  Upward: increased (×2)
  Downward: declined slightly; fell

  Text 2
  Upward: upturn; rose
  Downward: were down; decreased; shrank slightly; dropped

  Text 3
  Upward: increased; rose; climbed; dramatic increase
  Downward: fell slightly

B Vocabulary

- Make sure learners understand the grid, i.e. ↑ indicates a large upward change, whereas ↓ denotes a slight downward movement. Do the first two items together in order to check this. In pairs or small groups, learners group the other verbs.

  Answers

↑	↑	↑/↓	↓	↓
to climb	to increase	to remain	to decrease	to plunge
to soar	to rise	unchanged	to fall	to drop
to jump		to level out	to decline	

- Proceed in the same way for this part of the task too.

  Answers

+	++	+++
slowly	steadily	dramatically
gradually		suddenly
slightly		sharply

- Learners make sentences using the information from the table. First they should decide whether sales are up or down and then whether the increase/decrease is small or large. It may be helpful to do this together with the following notation:

  Brazil: ↓ (+)
  Iran: +/−
  Uruguay: ↑ (+++)

- To make the task itself more challenging, learners should not use each item of vocabulary more than once. When they have finished, let them compare their answers with a partner, then check them as a class. Obviously, there is more than one possibility.

  Suggested answers
  Sales in Brazil decreased slightly.
  Sales in Iran remained the same.
  Sales in Uruguay soared.
  Sales in Singapore climbed dramatically.
  Sales in Sweden fell steadily.
  Sales in Peru rose sharply.

- For extra practice dictate graph lines to learners.

C Grammar

- This section focuses on the difference between adjectives and adverbs. Point out the difference in form and also in word order:

  adjective + noun (adjective precedes the noun)
  verb + adverb (adverb follows the verb)

- Before learners begin the exercise, ask them to look at the verbs in **B** and decide which ones can be used as nouns. (All except climb, soar, remain stable/unchanged.) Learners make sentences, transforming as many of the sentences as possible they wrote in the above task.

  ### Suggested answers
  There was a slight decrease in sales in Brazil.
  There was a steady fall in sales in Sweden.
  There was a sharp rise in sales in Peru.

D Speaking

- Divide the class into two groups. Each group looks at their graph and completes the text. When they have done this, regroup learners so that they are working with a learner from another group. They then dictate their text to their partner, who draws the line in on their graph. Finally let learners compare the lines they have drawn with the ones in their books.

12.2 Cause and effect

A Warmer

- In pairs, learners note down reasons for the rise or fall of sales of soft drinks. Set a limit of a few minutes and then collect suggestions on the board.

- Learners look at the map in their books and add any other ideas.

  ### Suggested answers

↑ (rise)	↓ (fall)
hot weather	wet weather
launch of new product	price increase
opening of new factory	competition
successful marketing campaign	economic recession
increase in tourism	etc.

B Listening and presentation

- The first time they listen, learners can tick off the reasons they hear mentioned.

- The second time, they should complete the table in their books.

 *Tapescript*

Extract one
We've had an excellent year in the UK with an increase in both profits and sales over last year. I think we can safely say this result is due to our mid-year promotional push, in which we visited almost 7,000 customer outlets in two weeks and displayed over 210,000 cases of Fizzo.

Extract two
I'm afraid we've had a rather disappointing year in Continental Europe. Competition has been fierce and sales of Fizzo have declined. Er, this is not only a result of the recession we've been going through, but also of the fall in the number of tourists in the Mediterranean countries and poor summer weather. Despite all this, we have still managed to make a small profit.

Extract three
Fizzo has performed very well in North America and both sales and profits are up again. These results are due to our Total Quality Management programme which has led to significant improvements in product quality, customer service and productivity.

Extract four
In Australia, sales have fallen because of the recession, competition and poor summer weather. Investment in new products means that profits have fallen too, but we expect next year's results to be better.

Extract five
Sales and profits in Africa were up this year. This was due to improved production facilities, along with launching Fizzo in new bottles.

Answers

Area	Sales	Profit	Reasons
United Kingdom	↑	↑	promotional push
Europe	↓	↓	recession, fall in number of tourists, poor weather
Americas	↑	↑	TQM programme
Australia	↓	↓	recession, competition, poor weather
Africa	↑	↑	new factory, new bottles

C Grammar

● Write on the board:

Sales have risen ... our new factory.

and ask learners to try and complete the sentence. Elicit the three linking phrases, *because of, due to* and *as a result of*. Ask learners to give you some further examples of reasons why sales (could) have risen, either using information from the tape or their own examples and then proceed in the same way for *sales have fallen*.

● Learners match the halves of the sentences in their books and then join them together using the conjunctions. (Check they have the right halves before they actually rewrite the sentences!)

Answers

1b 2d 3f 4e 5a 6c

1 Production is more efficient as a result of new packaging methods in the factory.
2 Distribution is more efficient because of our new centralized warehouse.
3 Customer service improved due to our new distribution centre.
4 Consumers have greater access to our products due to new vending machines on all railway stations.
5 Our market share has increased as a result of the advertising campaign.
6 450 employees lost their jobs because of rationalization of management.

D Speaking

● Divide the class into two groups, A and B. Give them a few minutes to look at the first table in their respective files and make some sentences using the information in it, e.g. *Sales in the United States increased as a*

result of the hot summer weather. They should also prepare questions to ask members of the other group about sales in the other areas.

● When they are ready, regroup learners so that they are working with someone from the other group and get them to ask and answer their questions.

● To finish off, check answers around the class.

12.3 Presenting information

A Warmer

● Introduce the topic by asking learners if they have been on any training courses recently and if so, what and how they found them. If your learners are in work, find out if their companies have an in-house training programme; if they are pre-experience they should make a list of the kind of courses they think companies would offer their employees. Then get them to compare their ideas with those in the book.

● If learners have problems with the different types of computer courses, give them examples of well-known programs, e.g. *Word* is a word processing program, *Excel* is a spreadsheet program, *Access* is a data base program, *Powerpoint* is used to prepare presentations.

B Listening and presentation

● Learners listen and number the points as they are mentioned.

47

Answers

Time of change at Marea   ☐ 1
Sales have increased   ☐ 2
Set up in-house training programme   ☐ 7
Installation of PCs   ☐ 6
Identify areas for improvement   ☐ 5
Increasing competition   ☐ 3
Took a hard look at the way we do things   ☐ 4

- Learners listen again and note phrases used to structure the speech. These are underlined in the Tapescript, which can be copied for learners.

Tapescript

Good afternoon, ladies and gentlemen. Welcome to Marea. My name's John Snow, and I'm the training manager. <u>I'm going to talk to you</u> briefly about our new in-house training programme.

<u>Let's start by</u> looking backwards. As you know, the last few years have been a time of change at Marea. Although sales of our products have increased dramatically, so has the competition.

<u>Last year</u> we took a long hard look at the way we do things here and we talked to all our staff to try and identify areas for improvements. <u>One of the results of this</u> has been the installation of PCs at nearly all workplaces. <u>A second one</u> has been the need for staff training, and that is why we have now decided to set up our own in-house training programme.

<u>Let's move on</u> and <u>have a look</u> at this training programme …

Photocopiable © Cambridge University Press 1998

C Speaking

- Divide the class into two groups. Each group looks at their respective file cards and uses the data to prepare a brief presentation. Working in groups of two or three, learners (from the same group) use the data in their file card to prepare a short presentation. Let them practise it within this group before regrouping learners so that they are working with someone from the other group. They then present their information to their new partner.

D Discussion

- Learners read the E-mail and establish what the problem is, i.e. the Project Manager needs to brush up his English for an important negotiation. Ask learners to suggest solutions and write these on the board. They can then compare them with the alternatives provided in their book.

- Take the first suggestion and ask them to think of its advantages and disadvantages, using the vocabulary in their books. They should make notes. In small groups they should then discuss the other alternatives and come up with a solution. A spokesperson from each group can give a brief summary of the discussion.

- It might also be useful for learners to reflect on their own language training.

13 Money

This unit, on the theme of money, introduces different situations where price is negotiable, and gives learners the opportunity to practise a basic negotiation. Problems of collecting money are also presented, and learners will have the opportunity to practise writing a chasing letter and making a telephone call to chase payment. The unit introduces the first conditional with time clauses *when* and *as soon as*.

13.1 Negotiating the price

A Vocabulary

- Ask learners to look at the situations in their books and establish the differences, i.e. in the situation in the bottom right, conditions are fixed, in the other two, they are negotiable.

- Elicit the type of things that are variable when a customer and supplier are negotiating the price of an article, e.g. delivery dates, quantity, method of payment, etc.

B Listening and presentation

- Play the dialogue and ask learners to find out what is being negotiated.

  Answer
  Discount and delivery date

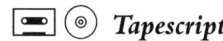 *Tapescript*

CUSTOMER: What kind of price did you have in mind?
SUPPLIER: The list price is $24,999.
CUSTOMER: That seems rather high for a good customer. Will you give me a discount if I pay cash?
SUPPLIER: I should think we can come to some kind of agreement.
CUSTOMER: Good. And what about delivery? When can you deliver the machine?
SUPPLIER: Well, we've got rather a backlog of orders at the moment. I should think it'll take somewhere between four and five months.
CUSTOMER: Hm. I was hoping for three.
SUPPLIER: Well, that's rather difficult at the moment. But if you're prepared to wait, we'll give you a reduction in price …

C Grammar

- See if learners can remember what any of the people said and write the model sentences on the board.

  Will you give me a discount if I pay cash?
  But if you're prepared to wait, we'll give you a reduction in price.

- Ask learners to look at the grammar box and establish the following rule:

will + verb	*if + present tense*
If + present tense,	*will + verb*

- Ask learners to look through the cues and go through the guided dialogue eliciting suggestions for each line. Drill these and then practise the whole dialogue with a learner yourself. Learners practise in open and then closed pairs until they feel confident.

- Finally, write up a model dialogue, with alternatives on the board.

D Speaking

- Divide learners into two groups and ask them to look at their respective file cards. Give them a few minutes to prepare what they want to say and then regroup learners into pairs.

- When they have finished their role play, put the As and Bs together and see who got the best conditions! Finish off by giving feedback on the use of language.

13.2 Getting paid

A Warmer and discussion

- Introduce the topic of getting paid by asking learners what they do when they get a personal bill, i.e. do they pay it immediately or leave it until the last moment? Discuss their reasons for this.

● If your learners are in work, ask them about their company's policy on payment, i.e. how long they give customers to settle an invoice and how long they wait before they pay their suppliers. Then ask all learners what would happen if nobody paid until the last minute. Use this as an opportunity to introduce relevant vocabulary such as *cash flow, agreed credit period, reminders,* etc.

B Listening

● Learners listen and complete the table.

Answer

Country	Agreed time	Average time
Sweden	30	48
Denmark	30	48
Finland	30	55
UK	30	78
Italy	60	90
France	60	108

Tapescript

PRESENTER: Bad payers are making life miserable for many of Britain's small businesses. As the recession and high interest rates hit company finances, many businesses are trying to improve their own cash flow by not paying their suppliers. Here's a report from Simon Anderson, our Economics correspondent.

ANDERSON: A new survey on overdue payments out this week shows that the majority of British companies are not paid within the standard 30-day credit period, but an average of 78 days later. Is this situation unique to Britain? Looking at the rest of Europe, the answer seems to be no. But it is only in France and Italy that the situation is worse. Italians take an average of 90 days to settle their

accounts; the French a grand total of 108. However, it is only fair to add that in both France and Italy the agreed credit period is 60 days compared to our 30 days.

Travelling further north, people seem to be better at getting paid. Like us, the Scandinavians have an agreed credit period of 30 days; in both Sweden and Denmark, the average period of payment is 48 days and in Finland 55. There are several reasons for this. Firstly, there are ...

C Reading

● Before learners read the article, brainstorm suggestions they might have as to how to make sure customers pay on time. (If you have time and your learners are interested in this topic, you could ask them to draft some guidelines.) Then ask them to look at the headings and match them to the correct paragraphs.

Answers

1c Check your customers' ability to pay
2e Set out your terms of trading.
3b Set up a system
4d Keep clear and accurate records
5a Collect your payment on time

● Learners reread the article and answer the comprehension questions.

Answers

6 Check with other businesses or ask for bank references.
7 Inaccurate invoices or unclear records.
8 Chase the outstanding payment.

D Vocabulary

● Learners reread the article, looking for words which fit the definitions given.

Answers

a credit
b promptly
c overdue
d delay doing something
e account
f chase

13.3 Chasing payment

A Reading

- Ask learners to read through the letter and find out why it has been written (to chase payment).

- Establish what information is missing from the invoice and elicit suggestions as to what questions they can ask to find this out (this prepares learners for the listening below).

  Suggested answers
  Could I have the invoice number?
  What was the date of the invoice?
  Could I have your customer number?
  What was the order for?
  What was the total amount?

B Listening

- Learners listen to the phone call and complete the missing information in the reminder and invoice.

- The completed invoice should look like the one at the bottom of this page.

Tapescript

CHEZDOY:	Redress, good morning.
PATEL:	This is Tara Patel from Cotton House in Kidderminster. Could I speak to Mr Chezdoy, please?
CHEZDOY:	Speaking.
PATEL:	Ah, hello, Mr Chezdoy. I'm calling about an outstanding invoice. Er, that's invoice number 523 705 from 3 April.

CHEZDOY:	Just a minute. I'll check our records. Sorry, what was the invoice number again?
PATEL:	523 705.
CHEZDOY:	Ah, here it is. 523 705, 3 April. Yes, I remember. That was an order for baseball caps and belts. Total amount £1,050. Er, there's a note attached saying we're still waiting for the rest of the delivery. We've only received the belts so far, the baseball caps haven't arrived yet.
PATEL:	Oh, I'm sorry. I didn't realize the order was incomplete. Our new software automatically prints outstanding payments at the beginning of the month.
CHEZDOY:	Don't worry. But I'll send you a cheque as soon as we receive the goods.
PATEL:	Good. Anyway, I'm sorry again, Mr Chezdoy. Thanks for your help. Goodbye.

C Grammar

- Write on the board:

I'll send you a cheque | $\begin{array}{c} if \\ when \end{array}$ | *I get the goods.*

and ask learners if the two sentences mean the same thing. Establish that *if* means something is possible (i.e. the goods might not arrive); *when* is used when something is certain – it's only a question of time. Point out that *as soon as* has almost the same meaning, the difference is that with *as soon as* you are promising to do something immediately.

Invoice no.	: <u>523 705</u>
Date	: <u>3 April 199–</u>
Customer no.	: DO 4630

Item:	No:	Units:	Price:	Total:
<u>Baseball caps</u>	9607-52	15	£25	£375
Belts	5072-52	25	£27	£675
				£1,050

Payment within 30 days

Photocopiable © Cambridge University Press 1998

- Brainstorm suggestions as to why companies don't pay their bills on time. Learners can then compare with their books.

- In pairs, learners match the reasons to a promise and then write some sentences. These are all linked with *We'll send you a cheque as soon as/when ... .*

  Answers
  1f   2e   3b   4d   5c   6a

D Speaking and writing

- Divide learners into two groups and ask them to look at their respective file cards. Ask a few general questions to make sure learners understand the invoices such as *What is the date of the invoice? How long is payment overdue? What is the total amount due?* Give them a few minutes to prepare what they want to say and then regroup learners into pairs to do the role plays.

- Ask them to sit back to back for this and monitor language while they are doing so.

- Finish off by giving feedback on the use of good and bad language.

- As a follow-up, learners could also draft letters to the customers, requesting the outstanding payment.

14 Socializing

Socializing covers the subjects of gift-giving when visiting clients abroad, organizing a free day while on a business trip, and eating out. Food and drink habits in different countries are also discussed, and learners will have the opportunity to develop their food and drink vocabulary. Indirect or polite question forms are presented.

14.1 Gift-giving

A Warmer

● Make sure learners can name the items in the illustration and get them to discuss their answers in pairs or small groups. What is appropriate will really depend on where your learners are from. A few inappropriate items have been included!

B Reading

● Before learners read the text, write the three headings on the board and brainstorm any information learners might have about gift-giving in these cultures.

● Set a time limit for the reading and ask learners to skim the three texts to find out which culture they refer to. The reference to Muslims should point to the Arab world; that of Lenten colours to (Catholic) Latin America.

Answers
1   The Arab world
2   Latin America
3   Japan

● Check answers and ask learners to reread the texts and answer the more detailed comprehension questions.

Answers
1   Latin America
2   The Arab world
3   The Arab world
4   Japan
5   The Arab world
6   Japan

● Follow the reading up with a discussion on the etiquette of gift-giving in your learners' country.

C Listening

● Learners discuss the questions in pairs or small groups. While listening they should make notes on Maria Kelly's answers to compare with their own answers.

Answers
1   It depends on the company. Employees in large companies are often not allowed to accept any gifts.
2   Yes.
3   Give the gift to charity.

▭ ◎ *Tapescript*

INTERVIEWER: It's always nice to receive a gift from a business partner, but what is acceptable? I mean, when does a gift stop being a gift and become a bribe?

KELLY: Well, that depends largely on the company. In America, we've found that many large corporations have a very strict policy on gifts. At General Mills in Minneapolis, for example, employees are not allowed to accept any gifts of money and any present they receive cannot be worth more than $25. Many other large companies don't allow their employees to accept gifts at all.

INTERVIEWER: I see. But what should you do if your company does not have an official policy on accepting gifts? Is it best to keep quiet or should you tell other people about them?

KELLY: Well, if you're in doubt, I suggest discussing it with a colleague or supervisor and seeing what they feel about it. You see, if it's out in the open, no one can accuse you later of accepting a bribe.

INTERVIEWER: Uh uh. And what should you do if you don't want to accept a gift from a business partner? I mean, you don't want to offend someone by refusing their gift. What do you suggest here?

KELLY: Well, one solution is to donate the gift to charity. Obviously if you do something like this, it's only polite to write a note explaining what you've done …

(D) Speaking

● Obviously this discussion will depend a little on your learners' position and whether they have much contact with suppliers and other 'gift-givers', but encourage them to talk about their company's policy on giving and receiving gifts and, of course, any gifts they have received.

● If your learners are pre-work, the first three questions will not be relevant, but they can discuss the last three in a more general context.

14.2 Planning a free day

(A) Reading

● If you have learners who have to travel in their jobs, put them in a group to make a list of things they like to do in their spare time when they are in another city or country. Learners who do not have to go on business trips, whether because they are pre-work or because their job does not involve travel, should form a second group and make a list of the things they imagine business travellers like doing in their free time. Once each group has made its list, pair learners from the two groups off to compare their lists. If none of your learners travel for work, they should all make a list of what they imagine travellers do in their spare time.

● Now set the situation by telling learners they are going on a business trip to Budapest. Find out what they already know about the city and elicit any kind of information they would like to have before travelling there.

● Ask learners to look at the city guide in their books and ask a couple of questions to help familiarize them with it, e.g. *Where's a good place to go shopping? Does Budapest have a metro? Where's a good place for a coffee?*

● Learners look at the listings and find a couple of things they would like to do. Either get them to do this with a partner and then team up with another pair to compare ideas or ask learners around the class. Encourage them to justify their answers.

(B) Reading and presentation

● Learners refer to the city guide to answer the comprehension questions.

Answers
1 By train, tram or bus.
2 At three o'clock.
3 At the foreign exchange bureau.
4 In September.
5 18 52 2000.

(C) Grammar

● Write on the board:

What's the best way to the centre of town?

and ask learners how they can make the question more polite. Establish the use of *Do you know …? Could you tell me …?* to do so and point out the change in word order, i.e. the verb now comes after the noun:

Could you tell me what the best way to the centre of town is?

● Now write on the board:

What time does the market close?
Could you tell me what time the market closes?

and draw attention to the omission of the auxiliary verb.

● Point out the change in word order for indirect questions. In pairs, learners write questions for the answers in their books. While they are doing this, go around and help and check their questions are not only grammatically correct, but also appropriate.

Suggested answers

1 Do you know what the country code for Hungary is?
2 Could you tell me what the Hilton's telephone number is?
3 Could you tell me when the Hungarian Grand Prix is?
4 Could you tell me what time the foreign exchange closes?
5 Do you know how much a tram ticket costs?
6 Do you know when the market is open?

- Ask learners to read out their answers and then give them a few minutes to practise asking and answering in pairs. Then regroup learners into new pairs and get them to ask the same questions and any others they can think of about another city. If your learners come from different places, they should use their home town. If they all come from the same place, ask learners to give information about a city they know well.

Resource activity 6: My home town

- Use the questions at Resource activity 6 (page 84) (or your own if you prefer) and fill in the right-hand side of the sheet with answers which apply to the town or city learners are learning English in.

- Each learner receives a question and a different answer card. Learners then mingle, asking their question until they find the person with the appropriate answer. When they find their answer they should keep the answer card.

- Ideally, photocopy questions and answers onto different coloured card.

D Speaking

- Using the headings from the Budapest city guide, learners should create a city guide for the city they are learning English in or a city they know well.

14.3 Eating out

A Warmer

- This discussion should either be based on learners' own experience, or if they do not have to attend business lunches, their knowledge of what happens at their place of work. You could also contrast this with the normal lunch break with regard to time, duration, etc.

B Listening

- Find out what learners know about business hours and doing business in Spain. Then ask them to listen to the woman's story and note down their answers to the questions.

Answers

1 Three thirty
2 Three hours
3 Yes

- Play it again if necessary, and if it is relevant, let learners tell the class of any experiences they have had entertaining business partners or being entertained.

Tapescript

I remember the first time I was in Spain on business. I was at a meeting and it was going really well, the language was no problem, we were racing through the agenda and I was thinking this is great, I'll be able to fly home late tonight with a deal in my briefcase. And then my stomach started rumbling!

Well, I looked at my watch. It was one thirty. These people must eat something soon, I thought. Two thirty. I was getting desperate. Quarter to three. Do they really survive on nothing but black coffee and cigarettes, I asked myself.

Half an hour later one of my business partners got up to phone and check that there was a table at his favourite Basque restaurant just around the corner.

Finally, at three thirty, I had a small glass of lager and some olives in front of me and a menu in my hand. We then went on to have this amazing three-hour lunch, during which we concluded our deal, and I was actually able to get an earlier flight.

But I learnt my lesson. Now, when I go to Spain, I make sure I have a second breakfast around eleven so I can survive until mid-afternoon without having to eat my fingernails. And now I know why I can never reach my business contacts between eleven and twelve – they're all out for a second breakfast!

C Reading and vocabulary

- Ask learners to look at the menu and choose what they would like to eat. Encourage them to ask about items on the menu they don't know and use this as an opportunity to explain them, e.g. *Salmon is a kind of fish; ratatouille is made with different peppers, courgettes and tomatoes; mature cheese is an older cheese — it's quite strong.*

- Then ask learners to reread the menu and mark all the different ways of cooking food that they can find.

  Answer
  smoked   fried   roast   grilled   boiled

- You could also ask them to look for words to describe flavours, e.g. *bitter, sweet, mature* and see if they can provide any more before going on to get them to describe dishes themselves.

ⓓ Speaking

- If your learners are from the same country, brainstorm regional specialities and write these on the board. Ask learners to imagine they have to explain them to a foreigner and build up a description of one or two dishes, writing useful phrases on the board.

- Have the names of traditional and/or typical dishes on cards and hand these out to learners to describe, naturally without naming them. The rest of the class should try and guess what the dish in question is.

- With mixed groups, ask learners to describe a typical dish from their country — as they might well have to do to a business partner during a meal.

15 Revision and consolidation

A Grammar

This exercise reviews the main grammar points in Units 11 to 14.

- Give learners about 10 to 15 minutes to work through the sentences, correcting the mistakes. It is probably best if they do this in twos or threes as it will encourage discussion of the mistakes and how they should be corrected.

- Then go through the sentences together, trying to get explanations from learners.

  Answers
  a   This is the catalogue **which** we send to all our new customers.
  b   Mr Saloman is the sales representative **who** is responsible for Malaysia.
  c   There was a **slight** decline in sales in Eastern Europe.
  d   This was because **of** the poor exchange rate.
  e   In North America, sales rose **dramatically**.
  f   This large increase in sales was mainly due **to** new products.
  g   If you'~~ll~~ take 30, we'll give you a 15 per cent discount.
  h   **I'll** take 30 if you deliver before the end of the month.
  i   We'll give you another 3 per cent discount **if** you pay cash.
  j   We'll write you a cheque **when** you send us the invoice.
  k   Can you tell me where the nearest Metro station **is**?
  l   Do you know what time ~~do~~ the banks open?

B What do you say?

This exercise is a controlled review of the main functional language points from Units 11 to 14.

- Introduce the activity by asking learners if they can give reasons for company results and elicit what they remember. They should then look at the sentences in their books and find the appropriate phrase in the second column.

- Alone or in pairs, learners match the remaining functions to the words said.
  Answers
  1d   2f   3g   4c   5h   6b   7a   8e

- Check their answers and then elicit other suggestions for each function. If necessary, write these on the board.

- In pairs, learners write a short dialogue incorporating **three** of the above phrases. Either let them decide on their own situation or give each pair a different situation.

- Go round helping them while they are doing this. When they have finished, give them time to practise and memorize their dialogue.

- To round up, ask some of the pairs to act out their conversation to the rest of the class.

C Vocabulary

- In pairs or small groups, learners write down as many words as they can for each heading. Set a time limit of two minutes for the first heading and then go through answers, writing them up on the board. Proceed in the same way with the remaining two headings. To add a competitive element, allow each pair or team to score one point for each correct item (correct spelling included!).

- As consolidation, ask learners to use some of the words in sentences.

D Reading

- Discuss the pre-reading questions briefly with learners and use them as an opportunity to check vocabulary of clothing items and time.

- Learners read the article and correct the statements.

  Answers
  1 **A long-sleeved shirt** and a tie is usual for most work encounters.
  2 Punctuality is **expected**.
  3 You should present your business card with **both** hands.
  4 Office hours are from **09.00 to 17.00**.
  5 Banks are open **9.30 to 11.30** on Saturday.
  6 The best time to contact people is **early morning**.

- As an extension, ask learners to write a similar article about business practices in their country. Write the following headings on the board:

  Clothing   Punctuality   Business cards
  Office hours   (Other)

- In pairs or small groups, learners write a short paragraph about each item. When they have finished, ask them to show their draft to another pair or group or display them on the wall for everyone to look at.

E Listening

- Introduce the topic by asking learners by brainstorming the different kinds of transport in the city they are learning English in. Ask them which ones they use and for what reason, e.g. *How do you get to work? How do you go shopping?*

- You could also ask which ones they prefer and why.

- Learners listen and note down the answers to the questions in their books.

  Answers
  Taxi, bus, minicab, car are mentioned.
  Taxi is recommended.

- Learners listen again and note down prices.

  Answers
  1 RM25   2 RM1   3 50 per cent
  4 60 sen   5 RM150   6 RM1

🔘 ◎ *Tapescript*

MAN 1: You've been to Kuala Lumpur, Mark. Tell me, what's the best way into town from the airport?

MAN 2: Well, you can take a taxi or go by bus. A taxi'll cost you about 25 Ringgits. A bus is cheaper at 7 Ringgits. But they'll both get you there!

MAN 1: Uh uh. And what about getting around downtown?

MAN 2: I always take a taxi. They're really cheap. Most fares within the central downtown area are less than 5 Ringgits, although you pay an extra Ringgit for a taxi from a hotel, and an additional 50 per cent between midnight and 6 a.m.

MAN 1: Do you have to negotiate the fare, or what?

MAN 2: Not usually. Taxis are metered. Just make sure the meter is turned on! The only problem is during the rush hour or when it rains. If you actually manage to find a taxi, the driver often refuses to go to a congested area, but if you offer twice or three times the going rate, he'll usually change his mind! The way to avoid messing around is to negotiate an hourly rate to hire a taxi for 20 to 25 Ringgits. By the way, not all drivers speak good English.

MAN 1: What's public transport like?

MAN 2: Not bad. Some of the city buses and minibuses are air-conditioned and quite respectable. And they're very cheap. Minibuses cost 60 sen for any distance, ordinary buses start at 20 sen and increase with distance.

MAN 1: And car hire?

MAN 2: That's no problem. That costs about 150 Ringgits a day. And petrol is cheap. Last time I was there it was just 1 Ringgit a litre. However, I personally don't think it's worth driving yourself – taxis are inexpensive and parking is often difficult.

Summary

See notes on page 22.

📄 ***Resource activity 7: Cost of living guide***

To review indirect questions (see Unit 14).

- Copy the cost of living guide at Resource activity 7, page 85 so that each learner has only a part of the information.

- Distribute among the learners. They mingle and ask their questions until they have completed all the information on the chart.

16 Business culture and ethics

This unit, on business culture and ethics, provides learners with a chance to discuss the cultures of different companies together with other issues relating to work, including women in work. Modal verbs *would, might* and *wouldn't* are introduced and learners practise expressing probability, giving opinions and expressing preference. The unit includes a questionnaire for students to assess their own ethical standards at work, and this, together with the material on women in work, should provide lively discussion.

Further Ahead video sequence 4, 'The Solar Way', covers the themes dealt with in Units 16 to 19 of the Learner's Book.

16.1 Corporate culture

A Warmer

● Ask learners to look at the photograph. Would they like to work in an office like this? How does it compare with offices they work in / are familiar with?

B Reading

● Begin by explaining the term *corporate culture*, i.e. a company's way of doing things.

● Ask learners what aspects make for company culture, e.g. history of the company, nationality, average age of staff, product, etc.

● Give learners about ten minutes to read through the three texts and do the accompanying task. Ask them to mark their answers in the text. When they have finished they should compare their answers with a partner before checking them with the whole class.

Answers
a   First Direct
b   600 Group
c   Bosch
d   600 Group
e   First Direct
f   First Direct

● To finish off, ask learners which company they would or would not like to work for.

C Vocabulary

● In pairs, learners reread the texts and find words for the definitions in their books. If necessary, they should use a dictionary.

Answers
a lathe   b executive dining room
c management   d previous   e overalls
f to clock on and out   g shop floor
h staff   i egalitarian   j warehouse

D Speaking

● Ask learners to look through the questions and suggest a few more questions they could ask on this topic. Ask some of the questions around the class so that learners are clear about what they should be doing and then divide the class into pairs.

● While they are doing the task, listen in and monitor examples of good and bad language – and interesting answers! To follow up, either ask learners to change partners and report on their first partner or ask them to report back to the class anything of interest they found out.

● If your learners all work in the same company or are pre-work, they should imagine they work for one of the companies described and make up any information they don't have. (It might be helpful to give them a few minutes to prepare answers for this in pairs or small groups.)

- You could also extend the discussion by asking learners about their experience in other companies they have worked for – and perhaps what they preferred.

16.2 Everyday dilemmas

Ⓐ Presentation

- Introduce the topic by asking learners if they can think of any examples where companies have behaved 'badly'. If they need help in starting, give a couple of examples, e.g. the Exxon Valdez oil spill, the Union Carbide explosion in Bophal or more recent examples of other scandals. These will probably lead on to more! Then ask learners if, given the choice, they would work for these companies.

- Learners look at the talking heads in their books. Ask them to read what the people say and decide if they would work for the companies they are talking about or not.

  Answers
  1 no   2 perhaps   3 perhaps   4 yes

- For pronunciation practice, ask learners to think about how they might say these sentences, thinking about which words are stressed, etc. Give learners a model and have them repeat it.

Ⓑ Language in use

- Write on the board:

100%	*I'd work for*	
↓		
75%		
↓		
50%		*a cigarette*
↓		*manufacturer.*
25%		
↓		
0%	*I wouldn't work for*	

  and try and elicit different ways of expressing the different degrees of probability. Alternatively, you could write the exponents on card and ask learners to match them to the percentages.

- Draw attention to the use of *would* to express an imaginary situation: also the contracted form of *I would (I'd)*.

- Give learners prompts and ask them to make sentences, e.g.

  TEACHER: *arms dealer*
  LEARNER 1: *I wouldn't work for an arms dealer.*
  LEARNER 2: *I might work for an arms dealer.*
  etc.

- Then introduce the question form, e.g. *Would you work for a bank?* and short answers:

  Yes, I would.
  Probably.
  I might/Perhaps.
  Probably not.
  No, I wouldn't.

- In pairs or small groups, learners practise asking and answering.

- Alternatively, use the Resource activity below.

 Resource activity 8: Class survey

- Photocopy the questions at Resource activity 8, page 86.

- With a large class, divide the class into an equal number of groups. Give each group one question. Then regroup learners so there is one learner from each group in the new group. Learners ask their question in these new groups and record the results. They then return to their original group and tabulate the results.

- With smaller classes, give each learner a question and ask them to interview all the other members of the class.

- Before they begin, point out that the numbers at the top of the question refer to the degree of probability, i.e. 1 = Definitely; 2 = Probably; 3 = Perhaps; 4 = Probably not; 5 = Definitely not.

- Learners present their results to the rest of the class. Write the following on the board as a help:

All	
Most	
Some	*of us ...*
A few	
None	

- To finish off, allow discussion of any controversial areas.

C Reading

This is a light-hearted quiz to check on learners' own business standards as to what they feel is ethical or not.

- Introduce the topic by asking learners if they feel it is all right to use the company photocopier to make personal photocopies; if they show no qualms about this, point out that it costs the company money and if every employee did this, it could cost the company a lot of money! Elicit any other examples of behaviour which might not be considered ethical at the workplace and allow a brief discussion of this.

- Make sure learners understand the following items of vocabulary before they complete the questionnaire: *to pad an expense account, to pick up the tab.*

- Then give them about five minutes to complete the quiz on their own.

D Speaking

- Put learners into groups of three or four to compare their answers. The best way of doing this is probably to get a member of the group to read out each question and let the others give their answers. Encourage them to justify these where possible.

- To finish off, ask each group if there were any areas they really disagree on – and why.

16.3 A woman's place

A Warmer and vocabulary

- In pairs, learners look at the categories and suggest a few jobs for each category. Set a limit of about five minutes for this and then check answers on the board.

- Alternatively, write the jobs below randomly on the board or on card and ask learners to categorize them according to the headings in their books.

  Suggested answers
  Clerical: Secretary, file clerk, typist, …
  Government administration and managerial: Executives, senior manager, bank manager, …
  Personal, catering and security services: Nanny, nurse, kitchen assistant, …

  Production, transport and construction: Assembly line worker, truck driver, bricklayer, …
  Professional and technical: Lawyer, accountant, engineer, …
  Sales workers and managers: Shop assistant, cashier, …

- Finish off by asking learners which jobs are typically done by men and which ones are typically done by women in their country.

B Speaking

- This chart shows the percentage of women working in these job categories in countries in the European Union. As you will see at File 41, 60 per cent of all personal, catering and security service jobs are done by women.

- In pairs, learners try and match the job categories to the chart. Use this as an opportunity to review the language of probability presented in **16.2** by writing on the board:

  It's definitely … .
  It's probably … .
  It might be … .
  etc.

  and encourage them to use it while guessing the answers. Before they check their answers at File 41 (p. 118), let them compare their answers with another pair and try to justify any differences!

- You could also ask learners to discuss why there are these percentages.

C Listening

- Learners look at the statements and try to predict which are false and which are true. Again, they should do this in pairs or small groups. Then they listen to the interview and compare their answers.

  Answers
  aT bT cF dF eF fT

Tapescript

PRESENTER: Women have been the job market's big success story in the past twenty years. But as they have found jobs, men have lost them. This week we ask whether women have driven men from the workplace. Over to Ms Holmes.

HOLMES: In the past two decades, every country in the Organization for Economic Cooperation and Development has seen a rise in the number of women who enter the workforce. At the same time, the number of men in work has fallen. There are two reasons for this. Firstly, younger men have stayed in education longer; secondly, older men have been taking earlier retirement. As a result, in America, for example, 46 per cent of the workforce are now women. And if things continue like this, the typical worker in some rich countries will be a woman by the 21st century.

PRESENTER: Why are more women going out to work nowadays?

HOLMES: Most of the increase is a result of the way married women arrange their lives; in the past, most women stayed at home to look after their children; now they return to work as soon as their youngest child is at school – or often sooner.

PRESENTER: But is it easier for women to find jobs than for men?

HOLMES: Yes, but this is because in all rich countries, most women do just a handful of jobs, they're secretaries, shop assistants, cashiers, nurses, kitchen hands, nannies and so on.

PRESENTER: So women are not taking men's jobs.

HOLMES: No, not at all. But what has happened is that 'women's' jobs have expanded while traditional 'male' jobs have been disappearing. For example, women are less likely than men to work in manufacturing. So as manufacturing jobs have disappeared, it's mostly men who have been thrown out of work. On the other hand, employment in service industries has increased. And women have benefited from this …

D Language in use

This extends the language of probability introduced in the preceding section.

- Draw attention to the different ways of expressing an opinion and then ask learners to complete the statements so they express their own view.

- In small groups, learners compare their answers. Throw open to discussion any statements which are controversial.

17 Meetings

Greening the office introduces learners to a variety of environmental issues, starting with the office environment. Learners will practise discussing green issues in the office and making recommendations. They will also practise asking for opinions and agreeing or disagreeing with them. Reported speech is introduced, and a variety of activities allow learners to practise the use of reporting verbs.

17.1 Greening the office

A Warmer

● Either in pairs or as a whole class, learners brainstorm ways in which a company can become greener. List suggestions on the board.

● Ask learners to look at their books and compare their suggestions with these. If they are in work, find out if their companies do any of these or other things. Elicit points for or against these measures.

B Listening

● Learners listen to the proposals being discussed and mark if the second speaker is for or against these measures. Then play the recording a second time and ask them to make brief notes of the reasons.

Answers (first listening)
1 Against   2 Against   3 Against
4 For   5 For   6 For

Tapescript

MAN: I'm drafting some proposals for greening the office and I'd like your opinion, Maria. Have you got a minute?

WOMAN: Yes, sure. Go ahead.

MAN: Right, here's the first proposal. We should write to our customers on recycled paper. What are your views on that, Maria?

WOMAN: Hmm. I'm afraid I don't think that's a very good idea. I mean, I don't think our customers would like that at all.

MAN: OK. Next one, then. What do you think about using china cups instead of plastic ones for the drinks machines?

WOMAN: Sorry, I'm afraid I don't think that's a very good idea either. I mean, where are we going to wash them, we haven't got a kitchen, we'd have to get one.

MAN: True. Well, try this one. We should encourage the staff to cycle to work. How do you feel about that?

WOMAN: Oh dear, I'm sorry to be so negative, but I'm afraid I don't think that's a very good idea, either. Even if people bring their work clothes to the office, there's nowhere for them to shower or change. And you can't have people running around the office in jogging suits all day. What would our visitors think?

MAN: Hmm. OK. Now, fourth proposal. I suggest banning smoking on company premises. What do you think about that?

WOMAN: Yeah, that's more like it. I agree with you on that. It would actually be quite good for our image being in the health care business.

MAN: Good, I'm glad you agree on something! Next one, er, we should start sorting the rubbish in the offices. You know, have separate bins for paper, plastics and that sort of thing.

WOMAN: Yeah, that's a good idea, too. We could collect the paper for recycling, er, as long as we don't have to write to customers on it afterwards!

MAN: OK. Now, last one. How do you feel about using refillable pens instead of biros in the office, Maria?

WOMAN: Yes, that's a good idea. I agree with you on that, too.

Answers (second listening)

1 Customers won't like it.
2 No place to wash the cups.
3 No place to shower or change, and staff cannot wear sports clothes for business.
4 Good for the company's health care image.
5 No reason.
6 No reason.

C Language in use

- The language here should be familiar to learners (see **Unit 2**). Point out that the second exponent for each function is the more formal one.

- With a slow group, it might be helpful to go through the suggestions in **A** again and list reasons that speak for and against them in key words on the board. Otherwise, demonstrate first with a learner: give an opinion and ask a learner for theirs. To structure the task, ask the second learner to use a coin: if they throw heads they agree with the first learner, if they throw tails they disagree with them. They should give reasons for their arguments.

D Speaking

- If you haven't done so beforehand, brainstorm more ways of greening the office/school. Encourage learners to talk about measures which have been implemented at their place of work or, with pre-work learners, in their school, and any difficulties that arose; likewise, talk about those which were rejected and why.

- Get each learner to write down three measures they would like to see implemented on a piece of paper. If you feel they are all going to come up with the same ideas, then allocate different ones from the book or use the Resource activity.

- Then divide the class in groups of four or five learners. Each learner should try to persuade the other members of the group to adopt their measures. A total of three measures should finally be adopted.

- To make sure learners are practising the language of the unit, insist that when a learner has finished speaking, they must ask another to contribute by asking their views, etc., hence ensuring that everyone has a chance to voice their opinions. One way of doing this is using Cuisinaire Rods: assign each function a colour (e.g. agreeing = green; disagreeing = red).

Resource activity 9: Be green

- Photocopy the file cards at Resource activity 9, page 87, and the strips and cut them along the lines. Assign learners roles A, B, C or D and, in groups, let them think about their roles. Regroup learners into groups of four with an A, B, C and D in each group. Give learners a selection of exponent strips and tell them that they are to use these expressions in the meeting. Learners are free, of course, to use other exponents, but they must try to use all the strips you give them.

17.2 Reporting

A Reading

- Start by brainstorming the pros and cons of packaging goods in plastic as opposed to glass bottles. Do this either as a full class or give learners a few minutes to think about the issue in pairs or small groups.

- Set the situation by explaining that Evergreen, a cosmetics company with an environmentally-friendly image which makes medium-priced toiletries (soaps, shampoos, creams, make up, etc.), is trying to decide how to package its new bath oil. Discuss what learners think would be the best type of packaging.

- Then ask learners to read the minutes of the meeting and find out whether the arguments listed are the same as theirs.

- When they have done this, ask for suggestions as to what people actually said during the meeting and write these on the board.

B Listening and presentation

- Learners listen and compare what the speakers say with the minutes in their books. **N.B.** The minutes here do not report verbatim what was actually said but the general gist. Point out that it is usually not necessary to quote word for word, just the general intention of what is said.

- Ask learners to listen a second time and check if the minutes are correct or not. The following point is incorrect:

  Max says glass is easier (not more difficult) to recycle than plastic.

CHAIR: Right. Let's move on to the next point, er, that's the packaging of *Black Musk*. Would you like to start, James?

JAMES: Well, I think we should stick to plastic bottles. It's worked well with all our other products. And the advantages outweigh the disadvantages. I mean, plastic bottles are light, they're easy to pack, they're easy to transport. And what's really important, there's no problem with breakages.

CHAIR: Olivia, what are your views?

OLIVIA: I'm afraid I don't agree with you, James. This bath oil is going to be more expensive than others in our range and I think it's important to go for a more upmarket image. I think we should use glass.

CHAIR: Right. What do you think, Max?

MAX: I agree.

JAMES: Sorry, with who?

MAX: With Olivia. What's more, we ought to reconsider the whole question of recycling. If we're going to encourage customers to bring back their containers, glass will be easier to clean than plastic.

JAMES: But do you really think people will bring back their containers for refills?

CHAIR: Laura?

LAURA: Can I just say something? Has anyone thought about the question of suppliers? I mean, if we use glass, we'll have to find a new supplier. Our present supplier doesn't do glass as far as I know.

JAMES: Good point. So perhaps we should stick to plastic.

CHAIR: Well, perhaps someone could get some quotes?

LAURA: Yes, OK. I can do that.

CHAIR: Right. So OK. Now let's move on to the next point …

C Grammar

● These are just a few commonly used verbs for reporting speech. Point out the different word order and also the use of the gerund after *suggest* and *recommend*. Point out to learners the change of tense in reported speech. Generally, the tenses move back one, i.e. present simple to past simple.

I want to go to Paris. → *She said she wanted to go to Paris.*

In pairs, learners match people's actual words to how they are reported.

Answers
1d   2a   3f   4c   5e   6b

D Writing

● Divide learners into two groups and ask them to look at their respective file cards. Group A then reports the conversation whereas group B writes a dialogue. When they have finished, regroup learners into pairs (A+B) and ask them to compare their versions with their partner's original.

17.3 Cutting costs

A Warmer

● If your learners are in work, find out what measures their companies have implemented lately or are thinking of implementing in order to save money. You might also try and find a consensus on the most and least popular ones! With pre-work learners, ask them to brainstorm ways in which a company might cut costs. Here are just a few:
  - ask staff to work unpaid (!) overtime
  - close the canteen
  - cut training of company employees
  - close second factory
  - reduce the workforce by 50 per cent
  - rethink the product mix.

● For extra discussion, ask them to rank these items in what they think would be the order of unpopularity.

● Ask learners to look at the areas which have overspent and brainstorm some ideas for saving money; it might be necessary to point out that just cutting these items completely might well put a lot of backs up (customers, staff, etc.) and they should therefore try and come up with alternative ideas.

B Language in use

● Establish what kind of things the person chairing a meeting or leading a discussion has to do, e.g. make sure that everyone contributes, that people don't get sidetracked, summarize, etc. List these functions on the board, and elicit suggestions as to how they can be expressed in English. Then ask learners to compare their ideas with the language box in their books.

● Point out to learners that the expressions in the 'Interrupting' and 'Dealing with interruptions' sections are more likely to be said by participants in the meeting than by the chair. 'Just a minute, ...' could be used by the chair to deal with the interruption or it could be said by the person who is interrupted.

⊙ Speaking

● In this section, learners role play a meeting in which they decide how to cut costs at Phoenix. This will work best if different learners take on a particular area (Marketing, Sales, etc.), explain why they have overspent and present options for getting their budget back on target. The group should then discuss the alternatives presented and decide which one they wish to adopt.

● For the meeting, you will need to divide learners into groups of between four and six. Ideally, try and aim for six so that you can assign four roles (see File cards) and also appoint a chair and secretary. If your groups are smaller, learners will need to double up on roles, e.g. a stronger learner could both take the minutes and present options for a particular point. Alternatively, ask learners to rotate the role of chair and secretary within the group during the meeting.

● Put all learners with the same file card into groups and give them about ten minutes to prepare their arguments. They should come up with at least three options for each problem. Stress that just cutting a measure is not a viable solution; they should suggest alternatives!

● If you have a separate chair and secretary, ask them to draft an agenda while the other learners are formulating their arguments. Should they need help, suggest they use the points below. Remind learners to put them into a suitable order.
 – Any other business
 – Minutes of the last meeting
 – Cost cutting: marketing

 – Cost cutting: staff benefits
 – Apologies for absence
 – Cost cutting: sales
 – Cost cutting: overheads

● You could also ask them to try to memorize the exponents from **B**.

● When learners are ready, regroup them for the role play. Make sure that the aims of the meeting are clear (see above) and set a limit of about 15 to 20 minutes for discussion. While they are holding the meeting, make a note of good and bad use of language to give feedback on later.

● If you feel your chair needs a little 'handholding', write the exponents on slips of paper and give them to this learner. They should then make sure they use them all in the course of the meeting.

Ⓓ Writing

● Learners draft the minutes of their meeting. They do not need to list all the arguments, but should merely summarize the action to be taken as a result of the meeting. It may be helpful to photocopy the secretary's notes so that all learners have something to work from. They should go through these in their groups before they start writing.

● Put learners into pairs to do this. If you have a large class with several groups, you could display them on the wall when they have finished.

18 Processes

This unit presents a variety of company-related topics. Modal verbs *have to, must, can, don't have to, can't* and *mustn't* are presented in the context of describing employment practices and rules and regulations at work. Processes are described together with appropriate sequencing language and the use of the passive voice in the present tense. Finally, a brief company history is given and the passive voice in the past tense is introduced.

18.1 Talking about regulations

A Warmer

● Preteach the vocabulary items in the box by giving your own examples and referring to the pictures in the Learner's Book.

● Then put learners into pairs to discuss the questions in their books. Learners from different companies should discuss these questions as they are; encourage learners from the same company and/or department to talk about other companies they have known and previous jobs they have had. Pre-work learners could talk about working hours of friends or relatives; ask them to think of the advantages and disadvantages of these and what they would personally prefer.

B Listening and presentation

● Ask learners to read through the statements and check they understand the concepts behind them, i.e. if something is obligatory or if it is merely a possibility, etc. Let them listen to the tape and decide if the statements are true or false.

● After listening a second time, they should try and correct the statements which are false.

Answers
1F Employees have to work 140 hours a month.
2F Employees can start work at 7 a.m.
3T
4F Employees can do overtime.
5F Employees can take up to two days per month of free time.
6T

🎧 *Tapescript*

MAN: So when did you actually introduce flexitime?
WOMAN: About a year ago.
MAN: And has it been successful?
WOMAN: I think so. After a few teething problems. You know, people forgetting to clock off when they went home and things like that.
MAN: So could you tell me how your system works?
WOMAN: Well, everyone has to work a certain number of hours a month, at the moment it's 140. Within limits, we can choose when we work, for example we can start as early as seven in the morning and work as late as seven at night.
MAN: But you must have some kind of core time when people have to be at their place of work? Otherwise there'd be absolute chaos.
WOMAN: That's right. Our core time's between nine and twelve in the morning and two and four in the afternoon.
MAN: What happens about breaks? Coffee breaks and lunch breaks? Do you clock off for them?
WOMAN: Well, we don't have to clock off for coffee breaks, we usually just go and get a coffee when we need it, but we do have to clock off for lunch.
MAN: And what about overtime? I mean, what happens if someone works more than 140 hours in a month?

WOMAN: Well, overtime's no longer paid, but we can take free time instead, up to two days each month. That's quite useful, really. For doctor's appointments and things like that.

MAN: Have you introduced flexitime throughout the company?

WOMAN: At the moment, it's just in Administration. In Production they're still working two shifts a day, but they are thinking of introducing some form of flexible working time. A flexible week or something like that, but you should talk to the Production Manager about that. He'll be able to tell you more about it …

C Grammar

● See what learners can remember about working times from the tape, giving them prompts if necessary, e.g. *core time*, *breaks*, *free time*, etc. Elicit the concepts behind the speakers' words by asking if things are necessary, not necessary, possible etc. and draw up the following table on the board:

Necessary:	*have to/must*
Possible:	*can*
Not necessary:	*don't have to*
Impossible:	*can't*
Forbidden:	*mustn't*

● Ask learners to look at the table in their books. Make sure they are clear about the differences between *don't have to* and *mustn't*, i.e. 'not necessary' and 'forbidden'.

● Ask learners to complete the first column of the table with their own information. If they all have the same working hours or are pre-work, put them into pairs and assign each pair a different role, e.g. Marketing Manager, Receptionist, Production Worker, etc. They should then decide on the answers to the questions and fill out the grid with this information instead.

● Ask some of the questions around the class, encouraging learners to expand on their answers using modals where possible.

● Learners stand up and interview three other learners. Give them about ten minutes to do this. Finish off by finding out who has the best and worst working conditions.

D Speaking and writing

● Give learners this background about the company to help them decide what kind of regulations they will need: Canine Candies is a small company producing high-quality chocolates of canine theme which it markets to dog-lovers through its mail-order business. It has a full-time workforce of 50, but in busier times of year (e.g. the run up to Christmas) needs to take on as many extra staff again.

● Ask learners to look at the topics listed in their books and brainstorm some of the factors involved, e.g. shifts for production; times when staff can or cannot take holiday; hygiene pertaining to producing edibles, etc.

● In small groups, learners should draw up between two and four regulations for each topic. You could get them to do this on large sheets of paper and then display them on the wall for all groups to look at.

18.2 Describing a process

A Warmer and vocabulary

● In pairs, learners try to label the parts of the car.

Answers

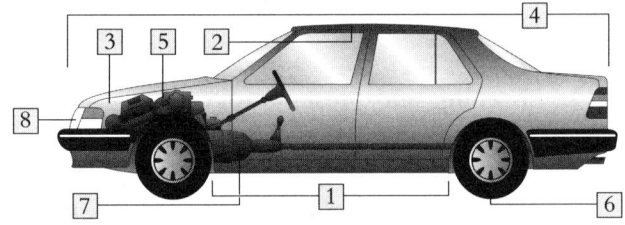

1 Underbody   2 Roof   3 Front wing
4 Body   5 Engine   6 Wheels
7 Gearbox   8 Headlights

B Reading and presentation

● Begin by finding out if learners know how a car is made. Use this as a chance to preteach the following items if you think they will not be familiar with them: *adjust, remove, fit, add, assemble, weld*.

● Learners look at the diagram in their books and see if they can work out the process. Then they match the text to the pictures.

Answers
1f   2h   3d   4g   5c   6b   7e   8a

C Grammar

- Ask learners to look at the grammar box and elicit how the passive is formed.

- Write on the board:

  | It is | verb+ed (past participle) |
  | They are | |

- For extra practice ask learners to reread the text and underline all the passive forms. Ask them to give you the base form of the verbs and vice versa.

- Before learners start this exercise, check they know the past participle forms of the verbs in the box.

  Suggested answers
  The radio is assembled in Korea.
  The tires are produced from Malaysian rubber.
  The cellular phone is produced in Thailand.
  The bumper is imported from Mexico.

D Speaking

- Learners should prepare notes on a process they are familiar with. If they are in work, it need not necessarily be a manufacturing process – order processing, invoicing or job recruitment, for example, will do just as well. Pre-work learners should describe a process they are familiar with – it need not be work related. Using a public telephone or withdrawing cash from a cash machine are just a couple of ideas.

- It is probably helpful to set a target of between six and ten steps in the process – so if necessary learners should simplify it. Before they start, write on the board:

  First …

  and elicit other items to be used for sequencing.

18.3 Company history

A Listening

- As the listening task involves listening for dates, check that learners recognize them by dictating a few dates and/or eliciting dates from them, for example, the year they were born, the year they started learning English, the year they joined their present company, etc.

- If *Hershey*'s chocolate is available in the country you are teaching in, find out whether your learners know (or eat) it and anything they know about the company.

- Ask learners to look at the artwork and texts in their books before listening to introduce and preteach some of the vocabulary. Then play the tape and ask learners to fill in the missing dates.

  Answers
  1 1886   2 1900   3 1905   4 1906
  5 1907   6 1925   7 1927

Tapescript

Good morning everyone and welcome to Hershey!

I'm going to tell you something about the history of the Hershey company before we go off and find out how chocolate is really made.

Let's start by going back over a hundred years in time. Did you know that chocolate was a real luxury then? Something that only rich people could afford to buy? So how come we all eat it today? We have Milton S. Hershey, the founder of Hershey to thank for that. He had a dream. And his dream was to make good chocolate that didn't cost a lot of money.

One of Mr Hershey's first businesses was the Lancaster Caramel Company. This business was founded in 1886 and was very successful. But when Mr Hershey saw some German chocolate manufacturing machinery at the World's Columbian Exposition in Chicago in 1893, he decided he wanted to make chocolate himself.

In 1900, Mr Hershey sold the Lancaster Caramel Company for $1 million. He used the money from this sale to build what is now the world's largest chocolate manufacturing plant. The completion of the Hershey chocolate factory in 1905 meant the mass production of chocolate could begin.

Mr Hershey's chocolate business flourished and so did the community around it. A bank, a department store, a school and even a zoo were built in rapid succession and in 1906 the village of Derry Church was renamed Hershey after its founder, Milton S. Hershey.

Many of Hershey's major products date back to these early years. *Hershey's Kisses*, for example, were first manufactured in 1907 and the *Mr Goodbar* chocolate bar was introduced in 1925. Then in 1927 the Hershey Chocolate Company was renamed the Hershey Chocolate Corporation and listed on the New York Stock Exchange for the first time …

B Grammar

- Remind learners how the passive is formed (see previous lesson) and show how the different tenses are formed by changing the tense of the auxiliary verb.

- Write on the board:

  It was
  They were | verb+ed (past participle)

- Learners make sentences about the information in **A**, using the verbs in the box to help them.

  Answers
  1 The Lancaster Caramel Company was founded in 1886.
  2 The Lancaster Caramel Company was sold in 1900.
  3 The new Hershey's factory was completed in 1905.
  4 The village of Derry Church was renamed in 1906.

5 *Hershey's Kisses* were first manufactured in 1907.
6 *Mr Goodbar* was introduced in 1925.
7 The company was listed on the New York Stock Exchange in 1927.

- Point out how questions are formed:

  Was it
  Were they | verb+ed (past participle)

- In pairs, learners practise asking and answering questions about Hershey.

C Writing

- Learners look at the fact sheet and, in pairs or small groups, draft a customer information sheet using the information on it. When they have finished, ask them to show their draft to another pair or group. Finally, they can compare it with this official version. You could also ask learners to read it and underline all the examples of the passive.
  N.B. If you are short of time, set this task for homework and go onto the speaking activity in **D**.

  Model answer

HERSHEY'S KISSES CHOCOLATES

Hershey's Kisses chocolates, a little product with a big future, were first introduced in 1907.

The basic concept of the present day **Hershey's Kisses'** wrapping machines dates back to a wrapper developed in August 1921. The familiar **Hershey's Kisses** flag was added to the product at this time. Before these automated wrapping machines, **Hershey's Kisses** were individually hand-wrapped.

Today's wrapping machines can wrap up to 1300 **Hershey's Kisses** a minute. Hershey Chocolates USA can make up to 33 million **Hershey's Kisses** per day, or more than 12 billion a year.

The production of **Hershey's Kisses** has been interrupted only once since 1907. The chocolates were not produced from 1942 to 1949 due to the rationing of silver foil during and after World War II.

Hershey's Kisses were wrapped in colored foil other than silver for the first time in 1962. Red, green and silver **Hershey's Kisses** were available during the Christmas season in addition to the year-round silver wrapped ones.

Today, **Hershey's Kisses** are 'dressed up' on a number of seasonal occasions. During Easter, the product is available in pastel blue, pink and green foil. For Valentine's Day, red and silver colors are used and in the Fall they are available in 'Fall Harvest' in brown, goldenrod and russet colors.

Hershey's Kisses, a favorite of chocolate lovers, are the most popular packaged candy brand in the United States.

Photocopiable © Cambridge University Press 1998

D Speaking

- For pre-work learners, or learners who all come from the same company, use the resource activity below.

Resource activity 10: Company history

Photocopy the information provided at Resource activity 10, page 88, and distribute it to learners. Give learners a few minutes to read the information; they might even form groups in As and Bs to discuss it briefly. They should also think about the language they will need, and could use this opportunity to prepare their questions. Once learners have started the activity, go around the class checking their use of question forms and making sure that their language is appropriate.

19 Conferences

Unit 19, on conferences, is largely a task-based unit providing revision and consolidation of much of the material presented in the book. Learners will have to choose a hotel for a conference and write appropriate letters to book facilities, they will have to organize the conference programme and deal with correspondence and problems that delegates have and, finally, they will have to give a short presentation on the new product, based on information provided in their book.

19.1 Finding a location

A Warmer

- Introduce the topic by asking learners if they have ever been involved in organizing a conference or, failing this, attended a conference, and let them tell you about this.

- Set the scene by telling them that they are going to have to help arrange a conference and ask them to brainstorm in small groups the kind of arrangements they think will have to be made, e.g. inviting speakers, inviting participants, arranging accommodation, etc. Each group should write their suggestions on a piece of paper and then pass it on to another group after a couple of minutes. Let the next group add anything else they came up with to the first group's list and then get them to pass it on to a third group and so on. While they are doing this, help with vocabulary if necessary (see, for example, the *To do* list in their books). Keep going until each list returns to its original group.

- In pairs or small groups, learners then look at the *To do* lists in their books and decide upon an order for the individual steps. If necessary, preteach *venue* and make sure they understand what is meant by *joining instructions*, i.e. how to get from the airport to the venue. There may be some differences in learners' answers, but encourage them to justify them.
  #### Suggested answers
  1 Set dates for conference
  2 Find a suitable conference venue
  3 Book venue
  4 Draw up conference schedule
  5 Decide on social programme
  6 Finalize conference schedule
  7 Send out invitations to participants
  8 Arrange accommodation for participants
  9 Prepare conference folders
  10 Send joining instructions to participants

- If your learners have experience of arranging conferences, you could ask them how far in advance they would do these things.

B Reading

- Brainstorm the kind of things that may be important when selecting a conference venue and ask learners to compare these with the criteria in their books.

- Learners read the two advertments and try to find answers to the questions.
  #### Answers
  See table on page 73.

- Finally, ask learners which hotel they think is more suitable and why.

C Speaking

- Divide learners into two groups and ask them to look at their respective file cards. Give them a few minutes to prepare what they want to say and then regroup learners into pairs.

- Ask learners to sit back to back while they are making their phone call. Listen in and make a note of good and bad use of language to give feedback on when the activity is finished.

Answers to **19.1(B)**

	Arosa Kulm Hotel	Le Montreux Palace
Location	Arosa	Montreux
Nearest airport	Zurich – 2 hours by car – 3 hours by train	Geneva – 45 minutes by car – 70 minutes by train
Accommodation	44 single 92 double	240 rooms
Restaurants	3	2
Entertainment	Bars, swimming pool, skiing, hiking	Medieval dinners
Conference facilities	Full details on request	Meetings of 20 to 1,400 persons Twelve meeting rooms

D Writing

- Check that learners are clear about the information they should be asking for. In pairs, they draft their letter. Offer help if necessary while they are doing so. When they have finished, ask them to show their letter to another pair and ask for comments. Finish off by letting them look at the model below.

19.2 Organizing the conference

A Discussion

- Learners look at the list of items to be incorporated into the programme for the conference. In small groups, learners decide on an order for the programme and fill in the schedule. Learners could also add any

---

KEF Audio

MAIDSTONE KENT ME15 6QP
Tel: (01622) 672261
Fax: (01622) 750653

Arosa Kulm Hotel
7050 Arosa
Switzerland
21 January 199–

Dear Sir or Madam

We intend to hold our annual sales conference from 29 June to 1 July in Switzerland and are now looking for a suitable venue. Our requirements are as follows:

Meeting room for 40 people, complete with OHP, flipcharts and video. The room must have excellent acoustics to demonstrate our product.

Accommodation for 40 people. We would prefer to have all single rooms.

Please send us information on prices and availability as soon as possible.

Yours faithfully

Photocopiable © Cambridge University Press 1998

other events they think are suitable to complete the programme. This is an open-ended task with no right or wrong solution; learners should, however, be able to justify their choices. Conclude by letting groups compare their results.

B Writing

- With a stronger class, you could try and build up a model invitation together and then get them to compare it with the letter in their book (if they decided upon the Arosa Kulm Hotel, they will need to change the letter accordingly).

- In pairs, learners mark the words which need to be capitalized (with a highlighter or by underlining them) and add punctuation. Finish off by recapping, if necessary, capitalization and punctuation rules.

Model answer
See below.

C Listening

- Learners look at the two E-mails and decide what the problems are.

Answers
1 Jan Zednik wants to know who is paying for travel and accommodation.
2 Susie Tan wants to know if there is vegetarian food.

- They then listen to two voice-mails and decide which E-mail they refer to. Get them to make notes where appropriate so they can use the information for the task in the next section.

📼 ◎ *Tapescript*

Message one
This is Shena. I've just got your message asking about the catering arrangements at the conference. Er, there'll be a buffet midday and in the evening with a variety of both meat and non-meat dishes, so I don't think there'll be problems for vegetarians.

Message two
Hello. Rohinton speaking. I'm returning your call about expenses for the sales conference. Er, tell participants that we pay for hotel accommodation and transfers from the airport, but they're expected to pay for their flights. Actually, if you can get them to let you know when they're arriving, you might be able to arrange for some of them to share taxis from the airport.

Answers
1 E-mail 2   2 E-mail 1

D Writing

- Learners draft replies to the E-mails. Alternatively, they could draft and then record voice-mails as replies.

KEF Audio
MAIDSTONE KENT ME15 6QP
Tel: (01622) 672261
Fax: (01622) 750653

Yoshi Watenabe
2-9-9 Shinjuku, Shinjuku-ku
Toyko 160
Japan

23 February 199–

Dear Yoshi

We would like to invite you to join us for the annual sales conference and launch of the new KEF loudspeaker range at Montreux, Switzerland from 29 June to 1 July. We enclose brochures on our new range together with a conference programme. Please let us know if you wish to attend as soon as possible.

Best wishes

Photocopiable © Cambridge University Press 1998

19.3 Presenting your product

A Discussion

- Start your class off by asking learners to recall a talk or presentation they have attended or, if they give them themselves, one they have made. In small groups, they discuss the questions in their books. If necessary, emphasize that it is not only content of the presentation which is important but also body language, gestures, delivery (speed, clarity), etc. You might need to give a few (negative) examples yourself to get the ball rolling; learners will then probably come up with their own anecdotes.

- An optional extra is to ask each group to draw up a list of **do's** and **don'ts** for would-be presenters, e.g.:

  Face your audience as much as possible
  Talk, don't read
  Show pictures, not words
  etc.

B Reading

- The aim of this reading is to provide input for the presentation in the next section. For this reason, it is not particularly technical.

- Before they actually look at the article, you might like to ask learners what they think is of importance for potential buyers of loudspeakers. Ask them to look at the article and find out what they think of the two loudspeakers depicted there and to give you their names.

  Answer
  Celeste and RDM Two

- Give learners about five minutes to read through the article and answer the comprehension questions.

  Answers
  1 Raymond Cooke.
  2 Yes (it was).
  3 It started using computer assisted design.
  4 The life-like sound of the speakers and the excellent performance and beautiful design.
  5 330 × 234 × 250 mm

C Speaking and writing

- Divide learners into pairs or small groups for this stage.

- They should use the information in the brochure as a basis for their presentation, but stress they do not need to use all of it and they are welcome to include their own ideas.

- Make sure learners are clear about the points they should cover in their presentation and remind them, if necessary, of the importance of structuring it by using 'signposting' language (see **12.3**).

- Weaker groups should write out their presentation in full and then mark their script for key words and phrases. Give stronger learners a blank piece of card (A6) and get them to make notes on this. Give them a chance to practise their presentation before moving on to the next stage.

  Option
- If you would like your class to work on different presentations, ask some learners to present the conference schedule (see **19.2**). They can keep to the same basic structure, i.e. welcome, introducing themselves, closing, etc., but the content will be based on the schedule they decided upon in the previous unit.

D Speaking

- Ideally, learners should work in groups of four or five for this stage. Try to set up the groups so that they are not working with learners from the previous stage. This will ensure that they are listening to a variety of presentations.

- While a learner is giving their presentation, assign members of the audience different tasks, using the ideas below or any other points that arose during the discussion in **A**. They should then give the presenter feedback and comments on the various aspects at the end of their talk.

Listen to another learner's presentation. Make a note of any *signposting* language they use.
Listen to another learner's presentation. Do they make *eye contact* with the audience? Or do they read their script?
Listen to another learner's presentation. Watch their *body language*. What *gestures* do they use?
Listen to another learner's presentation. Do they *speak clearly*? Or do they talk too fast?
Listen to another learner's presentation. Ask a question at the end.
Listen to another learner's presentation. Ask a question at the end.

- Finally, make sure learners take on a different task each time they listen to a presentation.

20 Revision and consolidation

Ⓐ Grammar

This exercise reviews the main grammar points in the last four units.

● Give learners about 10 to 15 minutes to work through the sentences, correcting the mistakes. It is probably best if they do this in twos or threes, as it will encourage discussion of the mistakes and how they should be corrected.

● Then go through the sentences together, trying to get explanations from learners.

Answers

a I **would** definitely not make personal calls from the office.
b I **probably** wouldn't send personal letters by my E-mail.
c I **don't** expect that prices will go up next year.
d Mr Tanaka **told** me that he's not satisfied with our present supplier.
e He suggested look**ing** for a new one.
f I told him I **don't** agree with that.
g He asked me **to** get some quotes.
h Most of our output is export**ed** to Central Europe.
i Some of our models are also **sold** in the States.
j The factory was complet**ed** five years ago.
k Last year more than 200,000 cars **were** produced here.

Ⓑ What do you say?

This exercise is a controlled review of the main functional language points from the first four units.

● Introduce the activity by asking learners how they ask someone for an opinion and elicit what they remember. They should then look at the sentences in their books and find the appropriate phrase in the second column.

● Alone or in pairs, learners match the remaining functions to the words said.

Answers
1h 2a 3f 4c 5e 6g 7b 8d

● Check their answers and then elicit other suggestions for each function. If necessary, write these on the board.

● In pairs, learners write a short dialogue incorporating **three** of the above phrases. Either let them decide on their own situation or give each pair a different situation.

● Go round helping them while they are doing this. When they have finished, give them time to practise and memorize their dialogue.

● To round up, ask some of the pairs to act out their conversation to the rest of the class.

Ⓒ Vocabulary

● In pairs or small groups learners categorize the words and find a suitable heading.

Suggested answers

Sequencer	Parts of car	Process verbs	Conference equipment
first	engine	fit	OHP
then	wing	assemble	flipchart
finally	body	add	video

● Ask learners to add a few more words to each category. To round off, ask them to use some of the words in a sentence.

Ⓓ Listening

● Ask learners to look at the chart and ask a few questions to check comprehension, e.g. *How long does it take to produce a car in America? Do many people work in teams there? How much time do they spend on training?* etc. You could also ask them to guess some of the figures for Europe and Japan, i.e. if they think they will be higher or lower than in the United States.

- If you have two rooms available, you could do this as a jigsaw listening: divide the class into two groups. Group A listens to the first extract and group B listens to the second extract. In pairs (A+B), learners then exchange information to complete the chart.

- The completed chart should look like the one at the bottom of the page.

- Round off by asking learners if there is anything they find surprising about the chart.

Tapescript

One

INTERVIEWER:	How long does it take to produce a car in Japan?
MAN:	About 16.8 hours.
INTERVIEWER:	And what about quality? How many defects are there per 100 cars?
MAN:	On average, 60, although we're trying to reduce this figure.
INTERVIEWER:	Could you tell me something about the way you organize your workforce?
MAN:	Teamwork is very important to us; we try to do as much as possible in teams. At present I'd say about 70 per cent of the workforce are organized into teams. I think one of the benefits of this is that our workers also make a lot of suggestions for improvement. We get an average of 62 suggestions per worker per year.
INTERVIEWER:	How many different job classifications do you have in the factory?
MAN:	Twelve.
INTERVIEWER:	And what about training? How much time do you spend training new workers?
MAN:	Training is very important. We spend an average of about 380 hours training a new worker.
INTERVIEWER:	What percentage of the production process is automated?
MAN:	The welding process is most fully automated. About 86 per cent of that is done by robots. Just over half – er 55 per cent, to be exact – of the painting process and just 2 per cent of the assembly process is automated. It's still early days, but we're hoping to automate up to 50 per cent of the final assembly process as, on the one hand, it's difficult for us to find young people who are prepared to work in factories and, on the other hand, we think automation makes factories nicer places to work in. However, it's not only the most labour-intensive part of the factory, but also the trickiest to automate.

Three approaches to car making	Japan	USA	Europe
Performance			
Productivity (hours per car)	16.8	25.1	36.2
Quality (defects per 100 cars)	60	82	97
Employees			
Workforce in teams (per cent)	70	17.3	0.6
Suggestions (per employee per year)	62	0.4	0.4
Number of job classifications	12	67	15
Training of new workers (hours)	380	46	197
Automation (per cent of process automated)			
Welding	86	76	77
Painting	55	34	38
Assembly	2	1	3

Two

INTERVIEWER: How long does it take to produce a car in Europe?

MAN: At present, an average of 36.2 hours.

INTERVIEWER: And what about quality? How many defects are there per 100 cars?

MAN: We reckon on about 97.

INTERVIEWER: Could you tell me something about the way you organize your workforce?

MAN: Teamwork is not a big issue here in Europe. At the moment, only about 0.6 per cent of the workforce are organized into teams. This shows in that we don't get many suggestions for improvement from our workers; it works out at something like 0.4 per employee per year.

INTERVIEWER: How many different job classifications do you have in the factory?

MAN: Fifteen.

INTERVIEWER: And what about training? How much time do you spend training new workers?

MAN: Quite a lot, on average it works out at 197 hours per new employee.

INTERVIEWER: What percentage of the production process is automated?

MAN: About 77 per cent of the welding process, 38 per cent of the painting and 3 per cent of the assembly process at the moment.

E Reading

● Brainstorm what learners know about Pirelli. Then ask them to read the article and answer the comprehension questions.

Answers

1 High performance tyres for Jaguar and BMW.

2 Japanese Institute of Plant Maintenance TPM (Total Productive Maintenance) award.

3 Teamwork and making teams responsible for the maintenance of their own machines.

● Learners reread the article and match the percentages to what they refer to.

Answers

1e 2d 3b 4c 5a

Summary

See notes on page 22.

Resource activities

RESOURCE ACTIVITY 1   Unit 1.1D   Introductions

CLAUS/CLAUDIA KOCH

Austria

Sales Manager

PAULO/PAULA BERTOLI

Italy

Buyer

**MARTIN/
MARTINE BERNARD**

France

Training Officer

**RICARDO/
MARIA DA SILVA**

Argentina

Marketing Manager

SIMON/TANSY WONG

Taiwan

Computer Programmer

JUN/KUMIKO OKUNO

Japan

Production Manager

Photocopiable © Cambridge University Press 1998

DRÄGERWERK

Drägerwerk AG, Lübeck, Germany, is one of the world's leading manufacturers of life-saving equipment and systems. It operates in the following areas:

Medical Technology
Safety Technology
Aerospace Technology
Underwater Technology

Drägerwerk employs 7,844 people in its Lübeck headquarters and in 30 subsidiaries around the world.

INKOM-BANK

We are one of the leading Russian banks and provide full banking services through 64 branches and agencies in Russia and a branch in Cyprus. We also have our own offices in Austria, Germany and Switzerland.

We employ 5,000 people.

Photocopiable © Cambridge University Press 1998

Find someone who:

1   .... has more than two children.

2   .... has an unusual hobby.

3   .... collects something.

4   .... is interested in ... .

5   .... isn't interested in sport.

6   .... likes listening to classical music.

7   .... plays an instrument.

8   .... has seen a good film in the last month.

9   .... has read a good book this year.

10   .... has been to a concert recently.

Photocopiable © Cambridge University Press 1998

business card	envelope
marketing manager	sales representative
price list	brochure
typewriter	computer
order form	check/cheque
telephone	fax machine
receptionist	secretary
calendar	diary
colleague	competitor
file	phone pad

Photocopiable © Cambridge University Press 1998

Could you tell me the best way into town?	
Do you know what time the shops shut on a Thursday?	
Excuse me, could you tell me where I can change some money?	
Do you know where I can get a quick snack?	
Could you recommend a hotel near the station?	
Do you know where I could get a present for my boss?	
Could you tell me where I can buy metro tickets?	
Do you know what time the banks shut?	

Photocopiable © Cambridge University Press 1998

COST OF LIVING GUIDE	
	Ringgits
Taxi from airport to downtown	25
Bus from airport to downtown	7
3 km taxi ride	5
Single room with bath in 3-star hotel	200
Single room in luxury hotel	
Lunch for two in average restaurant	
Dinner for two in average restaurant	
Dinner for two in upmarket restaurant	
Cost of 3-minute local telephone call	

COST OF LIVING GUIDE	
	Ringgits
Taxi from airport to downtown	25
Bus from airport to downtown	7
3 km taxi ride	5
Single room with bath in 3-star hotel	
Single room in luxury hotel	350
Lunch for two in average restaurant	
Dinner for two in average restaurant	
Dinner for two in upmarket restaurant	
Cost of 3-minute local telephone call	

COST OF LIVING GUIDE	
	Ringgits
Taxi from airport to downtown	25
Bus from airport to downtown	7
3 km taxi ride	5
Single room with bath in 3-star hotel	
Single room in luxury hotel	
Lunch for two in average restaurant	100
Dinner for two in average restaurant	
Dinner for two in upmarket restaurant	
Cost of 3-minute local telephone call	

COST OF LIVING GUIDE	
	Ringgits
Taxi from airport to downtown	25
Bus from airport to downtown	7
3 km taxi ride	5
Single room with bath in 3-star hotel	
Single room in luxury hotel	
Lunch for two in average restaurant	
Dinner for two in average restaurant	150
Dinner for two in upmarket restaurant	
Cost of 3-minute local telephone call	

COST OF LIVING GUIDE	
	Ringgits
Taxi from airport to downtown	25
Bus from airport to downtown	7
3 km taxi ride	5
Single room with bath in 3-star hotel	
Single room in luxury hotel	
Lunch for two in average restaurant	
Dinner for two in average restaurant	
Dinner for two in upmarket restaurant	300
Cost of 3-minute local telephone call	

COST OF LIVING GUIDE	
	Ringgits
Taxi from airport to downtown	25
Bus from airport to downtown	7
3 km taxi ride	5
Single room with bath in 3-star hotel	
Single room in luxury hotel	
Lunch for two in average restaurant	
Dinner for two in average restaurant	
Dinner for two in upmarket restaurant	
Cost of 3-minute local telephone call	3

Photocopiable © Cambridge University Press 1998

	1	2	3	4	5
Would you invest money in a cigarette manufacturer?					
Would you invest money in a manufacturer of junk food?					
Would you invest money in a manufacturer of alcohol?					
Would you invest money in a casino?					
Would you invest money in a firm which specializes in pollution control?					
Would you invest money in a company which specializes in alternative energy?					

Photocopiable © Cambridge University Press 1998

A

You are **for** these measures:

- no smoking in the office (you are a non-smoker)
- employees cycling to work
- using china cups instead of plastic ones

You are **against** these measures:

- sorting the rubbish
- using recycled paper

B

You are **for** these measures:

- no smoking in the office (you are a non-smoker)
- sorting the rubbish
- paying fares for employees who come to work by public transport

You are **against** these measures:

- using recycled paper
- employees cycling to work

C

You are **for** these measures:

- using recycled paper
- using refillable pens
- paying fares for employees who come to work by public transport

You are **against** these measures:

- no smoking in the office (you smoke 40 a day!)
- using china cups instead of plastic ones

D

You are **for** these measures:

- using recycled paper
- sorting the rubbish
- using china cups instead of plastic ones

You are **against** these measures:

- employees cycling to work
- paying fares for employees who come to work by public transport (it would be very expensive!)

I think we should ...	I don't think we should ...
In my opinion we ought to ...	I suggest ...
What do you think about ...?	How do you feel about this?
That's a good idea.	I agree with you.
I don't think that's a very good idea.	I'm afraid I don't agree.

Photocopiable © Cambridge University Press 1998

IBM

1911	–	Computer Tabulating Recording Company founded
1924	–	Name changed to International Business Machines
1930s	–	Name shortened to IBM
1935	–	Introduction of first electric typewriter
1952	–	Completion of IBM 701 – 19 sold for government/research

Ford

1896	–	
	–	Ford Motor Company founded
1907	–	Introduction of Model T car
1913	–	Moving assembly system
		Time required for chassis assembly cut from 12 hours to … hours
	–	Wages doubled to $5 a day
1916	–	Price reduced to $…

Ford

1896	–	Henry Ford builds first car in Detroit
1903	–	Ford Motor Company founded
	–	Introduction of Model T car
1913	–	Moving assembly system
		Time required for chassis assembly cut from 12 hours to 1.5 hours
1914	–	Wages doubled to $… a day
1916	–	Price reduced to $360

IBM

	–	Computer Tabulating Recording Company founded
	–	Name changed to International Business Machines
1930s	–	
	–	Introduction of first electric typewriter
	–	Completion of IBM 701 – … sold for government/research

Photocopiable © Cambridge University Press 1998